Albert Reville

History of the Dogma of the Deity of Jesus Christ

Albert Reville

History of the Dogma of the Deity of Jesus Christ

ISBN/EAN: 9783743332812

Manufactured in Europe, USA, Canada, Australia, Japa

Cover: Foto ©Lupo / pixelio.de

Manufactured and distributed by brebook publishing software (www.brebook.com)

Albert Reville

History of the Dogma of the Deity of Jesus Christ

HISTORY OF THE DOGMA

OF THE

DEITY OF JESUS CHRIST.

TRANSLATED FROM THE FRENCH OF

ALBERT RÉVILLE, D.D.,

MINISTER OF THE FRENCH REFORMED CHURCH.

An entirely New Translation, from the Revised and Enlarged
Edition of 1876.

LONDON:
BRITISH & FOREIGN UNITARIAN ASSOCIATION,
37, NORFOLK STREET, STRAND.
1878.

The British and Foreign Unitarian Association, in accordance with its First Rule, gives publicity to works calculated "to promote Unitarian Christianity by the diffusion of Biblical, theological, and literary knowledge on topics connected with it," but does not hold itself responsible for every statement, opinion or expression of the writers.

CONTENTS.

	PAGE
TRANSLATOR'S PREFACE	iii
PREFACE TO THE SECOND EDITION	v
PREFACE TO THE FIRST EDITION	xv

First Period.

FORMATION OF THE DOGMA,

FROM THE EARLIEST DAYS OF CHRISTIANITY TO THE COMMENCEMENT OF THE MIDDLE AGES.

Chapter I.
The Son of Man 1
Appendix to Chapter I. 16

Chapter II.
The First Disciples of Jesus 29

Chapter III.
The Doctrine of the Word 48

Chapter IV.
Ditheism and the Unitarian Protest 68

Chapter V.
Athanasius and Arius 96

Chapter VI.
The Dogmas of the Trinity and the Two Natures 125

Second Period.

ABSOLUTE DOMINATION OF THE DOGMA,

FROM THE COMMENCEMENT OF THE MIDDLE AGES TO THE EVE OF THE REFORMATION.

Chapter VII.

Catholic Orthodoxy 148

Third Period.

CONTINUOUS DECLINE OF THE DOGMA,

FROM THE REFORMATION TO OUR OWN DAYS.

Chapter VIII.

Protestant Orthodoxy.. 170

Chapter IX.

Antitrinitarians.—The Socinians 186

Chapter X.

Modern Philosophy 206

Chapter XI.

The Nineteenth Century 222

TRANSLATOR'S PREFACE.

In preparing an entirely new translation of this work from the revised and enlarged edition of 1876, I have, as before, considered it only just to the learned and eloquent author to be as faithful to the original as possible; and therefore I have endeavoured, according to his own request, expressed in a letter to me just before the publication of the first translation, "to make him say neither more nor less than he desired to say." In that translation some sentences were shortened, and a few passages, which did not appear necessary to the elucidation of the argument, were omitted; but in the present edition there is neither omission nor alteration.

Perhaps it may be considered by some persons that the French language is now so generally studied in England as to render a translation of any modern French book unnecessary. But the technical forms of thought of a history of theological opinions are not likely to be familiar in their foreign guise to even the most accomplished of English readers, while Dr. Reville is so distinguished as one of the leaders of thought amongst the liberal theologians of the French Reformed Church, and he presents his subject in so clear and concise a manner, that the publication of this, one of his principal works, in its present form, may prove acceptable, not only to the English public generally, but perhaps also to many of those who might be perfectly able to study the original.

My thanks are due to the Rev. Henry Ierson, who has kindly given me his valuable advice and aid while I have been engaged in the work of translating, and has carefully revised the proof-sheets for me.

ANN SWAINE.

June, 1878.

PREFACE TO THE SECOND EDITION.

During the seven years that have elapsed since this little book was published, it has been the object of criticisms, some very encouraging, others contemptuous, and others again decidedly hostile. We have been able to take advantage of them all in rectifying some errors of detail which had escaped our attention. But it had never been honoured by any systematic refutation. It was only a few weeks before the editor of the *Bibliothèque de Philosophie Contemporaine* indicated to me the necessity of preparing a second edition, that a fortunate chance brought under my notice the announcement of a *Refutation de la Christologie de M. Albert Réville*, by M. l'Abbé J. Troncy, Doctor of Divinity and Licentiate in Letters,* a respectable octavo of four hundred and seventy-one pages, which I hastened to procure, in the hope that the new edition might gain much from this reply.

I cannot say that the hope has been realized; I found only a controversial treatise. The Abbé Troncy is certainly an earnest writer, and very learned in his kind. Only that

* *Paris, Berche et Tralin,* 1875.

kind knows so little of what we now understand by impartial philosophical history, that it is very difficult for a man of religious and free thought to utilize the results of a research governed from beginning to end by the exigencies of an unreserved submission to traditional authority. We do not speak here of the form. We must rather thank M. Troncy for the comparative courtesy with which he has treated the author himself and the work which he desired to refute. That our narration should have upon him the effect of a "romance" rather than a "history"—this is a matter of course, and could not offend us. In fact, for him to admit that things have occurred as we have shown, would imply the complete subversion of the spiritual world as he conceives it. We are in his eyes "enemies of Jesus" (p. 2); our history is taxed with "falsehood" (p. 14); we have only undertaken it in order to "falsify" true history (p. 25); our reasonings betray "ignorance or dishonesty" (p. 257); we have "cunningly arranged the scenes so as to give distinction to a person" cursed by the Church (p. 438), &c.;—all this is neither true nor courteous; but these momentary slips of a pen usually more restrained, simply remind us of the infinite difficulty experienced by the disciples of the school to which the Abbé belongs, when the question arises of doing justice to the character of those who have shaken off the yoke of tradition. This is an old vice of orthodoxy, which has been too ready to think that all heterodoxy whatever necessarily proceeds from an evil heart. We must not be indignant on account of so small a matter: the fellow-combatants of M. Troncy have accustomed us to amenities far more rancorous. Let us come at once to the substantial question at issue.

The large volume, under which the Abbé Troncy flatters himself that he has crushed our modest duodecimo, appears to us to confirm in every part of it what we said in the Preface to our first edition respecting the illusions which the dogmatic or traditional mode of thinking necessarily engenders in the mind of one who undertakes to write history by its delusive light. Every moment the learned Abbé has had to show, with the indispensable aid of laborious explanations, how it happens that the ancient Christian writers taught the Trinitarian dogma, while at the same time saying numbers of things contrary to it. He cannot distinguish the various shades of opinion whose affinities we have carefully indicated while not omitting to point out also differences such as become in the end real points of opposition when stress is laid upon them, but sees in all this only one uniform colour. He does not always understand us, and, in the act of contesting our assertions, it often happens that he is, to use a common expression, breaking through doors already wide open. We think we have shown, for instance, that the orthodox belief of the third century might be briefly described as a kind of *Ditheism*, of which the God-Word, incarnate in Jesus, and God in the absolute sense, or *the* Father, were the two distinct and unequal terms. To what purpose, then, does our honourable opponent make an avalanche of citations to prove that the Fathers of that period admitted the divinity of the Word, its identity with the Christ, its adorable character, &c.? Have we anywhere disputed this evidence? What we have done, what our duty as a historian required us to do, has been to show, on the one hand, that these ancient authors were continually approximating closer in their theology to the subsequent more rigorous definition of the dogma of the Church; while, on the other hand, these points of similarity cannot efface the grave difference which still separated them from it, and which consists in this, that they all more or less formally taught the inferiority of the *Son*, or the God-Word, in comparison with the God-Father. No one of our citations has been proved false; the most striking of them have been simply ignored. We have therefore nothing to change in the views we have expressed upon this phase of the history of the Trinitarian dogma. The same thing must be said regarding the arguments which the Abbé has sought for in the *Acts* of the martyrs of the first three centuries,—documents, the origins, dates, and veracity of which are, besides, too uncertain for solid conclusions to be based upon their testimony.

We shall not make a detailed reply to the long refutation of which our book is the object. We have confined ourselves to introducing here and there, in the text of the new edition, some elucidations adapted to meet certain objections of the Doctor in Catholic divinity. The few persons whom this discussion may interest will easily recognize them. We have, however, made one exception to this rule—a rule imposed

Preface to the Second Edition. xi

by the very nature of a historical summary. M. Troncy has thought that he could without inconvenience shorten his task by limiting his refutation to the half of our little book. He seems to think indeed that, in order to show how far I err in laying down the principle as regards the dogma of the divinity of Jesus Christ, that a period of formation must be distinguished and another of decline, he has only to prove that my period of formation is imaginary, and that it will therefore be sufficient to refute step by step my exposition of the primitive history of the dogma from the appearance of Jesus up to the Council of Nicæa. According to him, all the Gospels, even the Synoptics, all the Apostles, even St. Paul, all the ante-Nicene Fathers, even Tertullian and Origen, must have shared and professed the belief that was afterwards defined at Nicæa, Constantinople, and Chalcedon. One ought not to speak therefore of formation, of fluctuations, of contradictions, where, in reality, one can only admire the stability of a doctrine revealed complete in all its parts from the beginning, and since then invariable. And consequently it were useless to pursue further the refutation of the "romance," when the purely fictitious foundation of it has been disclosed.

The Abbé was free to adopt this method, one certainly more expeditious than that which would have led him to demolish our brief history from beginning to end. We might ask him, it is true, whether, supposing it to be acknowledged that his favourite dogma is by degrees dissolving since the sixteenth century, it is not extremely probable that there should have been a period of formation equally gradual with this final decline of a grand belief. But we prefer to borrow from him his manner of simplifying the discussion. If then, for example, it is beyond doubt that in examining the most ancient documents which tell us of Jesus Christ, of his doctrines and his life, that is to say, the three Synoptical Gospels, we cannot find the least indication in the earliest days of the Church of a belief identical with that which afterwards became the Trinitarian orthodoxy; if from these documents it appears that neither Jesus himself nor his first disciples had the least idea of it; while four centuries later we see the dogma of his absolute deity imposed not without long debates upon the acceptance of Christendom,—it is very evident that there must have been a series of middle terms leading from primitive ignorance to the complex affirmation of later times. The whole question is reduced to this, whether I have succeeded in correctly describing these, as I still think that I have, while ready to submit to every scientific correction.

This is why I have added to the first Chapter an Appendix, in which I examine the reasons alleged by M. Troncy to show that the first Gospels, while quite silent, as he acknowledges, upon the metaphysical divinity of Jesus Christ, still make it the foundation of all their narratives, so that, if they do not teach it formally, they everywhere presuppose it.

However, I shall be excused if, in my turn, I do not carry further the apology for my historical review. It would require a book equal in size to that of my antagonist, and the labour would be but lost. I should not succeed in convincing either him or any of those who share his preconceived opinions. There are decidedly two irreconcilable ways of viewing history, the way of authority and that of independent thought. But what is to be said of one who can maintain seriously in pages of much learning that the Apostle Paul is the author of the Epistle to the Hebrews (p. 55), and that he always acknowledges Peter's right of primacy (p. 98); that the Second Epistle of Peter is authentic (p. 87); that the works of Justin Martyr abound in quotations from the Gospel of John (p. 154); that Tertullian has not taught the generation of the Word in time, and that his lampoon against Praxeas is not a work of ill feeling (p. 370); that Pope Callistus was a saint (p. 407); that two beings, one of whom possesses in himself the principle of his existence, while the other receives this from the first, are equal in perfection and in dignity (*passim*); that Constantine convoked the Council of Nicæa in concert with Pope Sylvester, and that this assembly was presided over by that Pope in the person of his legates (p. 445), and other things of the same kind? Such an author may undoubtedly teach theology with distinction in a "Seminary," but he ought not to venture into the domain of free science. He is not "a stranger in Jerusalem," it is evident; but he has put himself out of the position to know what has really "come to pass" there.

PREFACE TO THE FIRST EDITION.

RELIGIOUS criticism, long neglected in France, where however the seventeenth century witnessed its birth, has now for some years recovered its rightful position amongst us. I would not venture to affirm that there is any great number of persons who know more of it than the name; but it appears to me that a remarkable change, the natural effect of this revival, is gradually being introduced into opinion upon religious matters. The historical mode of thought is taking the place of the dogmatical. I mean by this that, instead of considering the doctrines of religion as so many absolute propositions complete from the beginning which must be adopted or rejected *without question*, men are becoming familiarized with the idea that the great law of natural development is not less applicable to them than to other terrestrial phenomena. They are therefore no longer astonished to learn that these too have a history.

The fact is, that nothing so falsifies history as the dogmatic or traditional habit of thought. It absorbs real diversities into a factitious unity. It takes no account of shades of variation, and it confounds different epochs. It makes of conditions full of movement, warmth, and decided contrasts, mere ground plots, laid out by rule, where everything is motionless and frigid. These illusions are not confined to minds in subjection to one or other of the traditions which divide amongst them the official control over the souls of men. There is not only a Catholic dogmatism, a Protestant dogmatism, and a Jewish dogmatism, but there is also a non-religious dogmatism, which is sometimes not less intense or less narrow than the others. No doubt an exclusive adherence to the historical point of view would only offer to thought a path without issue. One must arrive at a conclusion respecting the subject the history of which he has studied. But such conclusions ought to be supported and guided by that history itself, and this change of method necessarily influences the result sought for.

Perhaps there is no religious doctrine which justifies these preliminary remarks more than the dogma of the divinity of Jesus Christ. The proposition *Jesus is God* was till recently to all persons, except a few Unitarian Protestants, a kind of solid block that must be taken or rejected as a whole. It was supposed that no one could be a Christian who did not admit it. Jesus of Nazareth was conceived of as having claimed for himself the name and the attributes of the Divinity, as having founded upon this claim his right to be believed and implicity obeyed, and as having been the voluntary victim of an assertion which had reduced his countrymen to the alternative of either adoring him as the Creator, or putting him to death as a blasphemer. Even at the present day those of the Jewish theologians who are not initiated into the grand works of religious criticism, have no other idea upon the subject. By a strange vicissitude in things, their persecution under the absurd charge of deicide having ceased, some Doctors in Israel persist in demonstrating, as tenaciously as their predecessors formerly laboured to avert the cruel consequences which the ancient intolerance chose to deduce from it, that according to the true Christian view, the Jewish people did put a God to death.

So also scarcely any person doubted that the Apostles of Christ had preached the same doctrine, and that the Church, by its legitimate representatives, had officially taught it from the beginning. If those who were better instructed felt some surprise at the obscurity which seemed to them to prevail in the earliest expressions of Christian belief, they nevertheless admitted that the Councils, in defining the faith of the Church in such a manner as to dissipate all doubts as to its true object, had only expressed with greater clearness the permanent belief of Christendom. The maxim of Vincent de Leyrins, more boastful than true, *Ecclesia dicens nove nunquam dicit nova*, the Church, when it employs new terms, never says anything new, influenced the entire history of Christianity; philosophers and submissive believers were equally satisfied with it. Some of our readers will no doubt remember the amusing alarm of M. Cousin, when, in his first visit to Germany, he found himself unexpectedly, and precisely on this question of the divinity of Christ, in presence of the historical work already achieved in that country, the results of which overturned from the foundation all his theories upon the relations between religion and philosophy. They will also remember with what easy indifference the French philosopher freed himself from the difficulty. He adopted the resolution to take no notice of it, and, what is most amazing, forty years afterwards he still maintained that that was the right course.

This would be no longer possible at the present day. In Germany and Holland, since the appearance of the great works of the earlier half of this century on ecclesiastical history, in Switzerland, and amongst the Unitarians of England, and especially of America, many have long regarded this pretended perpetuity of the faith in its true light. In France a similar modification of the commonly accepted views will follow the investigations of which the person of Jesus is the main subject. It will be seen in future that the orthodox dogma of the divinity of Jesus Christ is one of the forms—perhaps the most logical, perhaps the best—I do not think so, but I do not at this moment dispute it—in any case, one form amongst many others of the Christian faith; that there is nothing primitive in it, consequently nothing essential to the very existence of Christianity; that not only Jesus himself, but the apostolic age and the two following centuries, did without it; that it was not formed complete in all its parts, but little by little, and under the influence of various principles, some of the highest order, and others not very exemplary; that, in a word, this dogma has a history internal to Christendom. If, therefore, even after having reigned in the Church for centuries, it should slowly disappear on our religious horizon, it is not to be hence inferred that Christianity is disappearing with it. Having originated without it, the Gospel is perfectly able to survive it, as indeed it survives already in the souls of numbers of Christians on both sides of the Atlantic.

It is the history of this dogma which we propose to sketch in this volume, offering as a guarantee for our impartiality this confession, that, while warmly attached to Christianity in its essence, that is to say, to the religious principle of which Jesus of Nazareth is the type and the introducer amongst men, we exercise a complete independence with regard to the formulas successively sanctioned by the dogmatisms of the past. What we hold to of these for our own part, is what appears to us to be true in them, apart from all supernatural authority. It has been said that, in order to write the history of a religion properly, one ought to be unconnected with it. If by this is meant that he must be emancipated from its traditional forms, the remark is correct; but if this disconnection means that he should have taken up a position of hostility to it, it is incorrect. On the contrary, I think that to relate any facts and clearly to explain any doctrines which are intimately connected in their origin with sentiments of a kind altogether peculiar, it is at least necessary to be in sympathy with the sentiments which constitute the groundwork of such a history. Absolute indifference does not belong to human nature. An ardent faith frequently obscures the mental vision; but can any one imagine that incredulity has no disturbing influence upon it? The impassioned attack of the "free-thinker," who believes that he is defending his freedom of mind against oppressive pretensions, does it less easily degenerate into special pleading than do the "apologies at any cost" of the believer? Let us seek for guarantees of impartiality in serene elevation, rather than in the direction fixed by some point of view that may be preferred. In the domain of the "Christianity of the spirit" to which we adhere, the love of the truth in history, as in everything, is the virtue proper for the seeker. On a ground like this, under whatever form the truth presents itself, it would be anti-Christian to disguise it, or knowingly to deny it.

Some further preliminary explanations are necessary.

In the language of theology, the term dogma is applied to a religious doctrine stated by those who are regarded as having the right to express officially the belief of the religious communion to which they belong. Once proclaimed, the dogma becomes something fixed and immovable; at least such is the pretension of those who promulgate it. It professes to express what is absolutely true. The Stoics designated by this word maxims defining the articles of the sovereign law, what we should call moral precepts.* In this sense, primitive Christendom had no dogma. It had no centre of unity for its enunciation. It was from the period of the definitive establishment of the episcopate, that is, since the close of the second century, that the word dogma was employed to designate the Christian doctrines. Its adoption by the Church coincides with the time when Christianity, contrary to the idea of its Founder, was looked upon essentially as an *orthodoxy*, a *recta fides*, a religion imposing upon its adherents as a primary and indispensable condition, the profession of correct doctrines with respect to the objects of faith.

With this explanation we proceed to state in a few words in what consists the orthodox dogma of the divinity of Jesus Christ. According to this dogma, he who lived on earth eighteen centuries ago under the well-known name of Jesus of Nazareth, is the second of the three Persons in the Trinity, THE SON, God with the same absolute title as the Father and the

---

* Comp. Cicero, *Acad. Quæst.* ii. 9 : *Quæ (sapientia) neque de seipsa dubitare debet, neque de suis decretis, quæ philosophi vocant δόγματα quorum nullum sine scelere prodi poterit. . . . Non potest igitur dubitari quin decretum nullum falsum possit esse, sapientique satis non sit non esse falsum, sed etiam stabile, fixum, ratum esse debeat, quod movere nulla ratio queat.* Ibid. 43 : "*Ne incognito assentiar,*" *quod mihi tecum est dogma commune.* Marc. Aurel., Εἰς ἑαυτ. ii. 3 : Ταῦτά σοι ἀρκείτω, ἀεὶ δόγματα ἔστω .—This philosophical acceptation of the word *dogma* no doubt proceeded from the custom of placing the words δοκεῖ, δέδοκται, *it appears right, it is decreed,* at the head of the judgments or decrees of the sovereign power.

Holy Spirit, excepting that he derives his existence from the Father by virtue of an incomprehensible generation. He has besides another peculiarity which distinguishes him from the two other Persons joined with him in the unity of the Divinity, namely, that the Son at a certain historical moment became incarnate in the womb of a Jewish virgin, and thus, without losing anything of his Divine nature, took possession of the human nature complete; so that he is at the same time, without prejudice to the unity of his person, truly man and truly God, *verus homo, verus Deus.*

Such is the doctrine which, having been slowly elaborated, arrived at supremacy in the Christian Church towards the end of the fifth century, and which, after continuing undisputed, excepting in connection with some obscure heresies, for eleven centuries, has been gradually from the sixteenth century losing its prestige, although it is still the professed belief of the majority of Christians. It is, I repeat, the history of this doctrine that we shall endeavour to recapitulate, which is all we can promise to do within the limits here assigned us. Elsewhere have large volumes been devoted to it; here we must confine ourselves to special points of time and salient facts, and hence our history divides itself into three periods. There is a first period of incubation and slow formation, which dates from the early days of Christianity, and ends nearly at the commencement of the middle ages; then comes a period of triumphant immovability, which terminates in the sixteenth century; and lastly, a period of slow transformation and decline, which commenced at the Reformation and still continues. Of these three periods, the second, although the longest, is naturally the least varied, and it will occupy less of our attention than the other two.

We have not only to contend against the difficulties inherent to every recapitulation. The entire history of dogma, and especially that of the doctrines concerning the person of Jesus, cannot easily be separated from the general history of the Church. In one and the same period, the dogma, the discipline, the worship, the moral sentiment, and the ecclesiastical organization, are closely connected together, and can only be properly explained by their reciprocal influence. Hence the indispensable necessity of our occasionally casting a rapid glance over regions adjacent to our special subject. However, this inconvenience, if it be one, will only the better serve to bring out one of those facts in the history of religion which most astonish those who have but little studied it, namely, that the religious sentiment has its own logic, a logic original and most rigorous. It is not in the least alarmed at contradictions; on the contrary, there are times when it might be said that it seeks and delights in them. But—and the point deserves particular notice—the contradictions, as well as the logically unexceptionable propositions, which proceed from the religious sentiment, are controlled by a *higher law*, by the law of its own interests, of its mystic satisfaction, of the demands which this satisfaction makes along the whole course on which this sentiment originally entered in the hope of attaining it. It is by obedience to this, its sovereign law, that it is so often unfaithful to reason. Mysticism, once set in activity, is not less subtle than scholasticism in gaining its ends. An enthusiastic religious sentiment shatters the common logic to pieces, as over-heated vapour causes the sides of a boiler to burst. But, like that vapour, it follows its nature, it obeys the law of its being. This observation explains beforehand how great an interest may attach to what at first appears to be merely a long series of wearisome subtilties, and it is eminently instructive to follow the inner logic of religious belief, even, or rather especially when it ends in the absurd. There is perhaps a pledge of the future reconciliation of independent thought and religious faith in the fact that, when we trace back to their root-principle the evolutions of beliefs the most directly opposed to reason or experience, we generally find that they have originated in a most pure sentiment, which has indeed erred in its course, but of which nothing of its primitive rectitude has been lost by its prolonged aberrations.

HISTORY

OF THE

DOGMA OF THE DEITY OF JESUS CHRIST.

FIRST PERIOD.

FORMATION OF THE DOGMA,

FROM THE EARLIEST DAYS OF CHRISTIANITY TO THE COMMENCEMENT OF THE MIDDLE AGES.

CHAPTER I.

THE SON OF MAN.

At the source of this whole history, at the point where all its variations begin, lies a sentiment of incalculable power, the sense of a divine ideal manifested in the word and the person of Jesus. Of this sentiment it is perhaps more easy at the present time to form a just appreciation than it was at the very moment when it first sprang up. Let us endeavour to arrive at a clear understanding respecting it.

Man is naturally religious; his history is the unanswerable proof of this fact. The religious sentiment, that intermingling in various degrees of awe and admiration, of melancholy and joy, of timidity and boldness, of fear and love, is awakened in the presence of whatever bears the mark of the perfect or the infinite, and especially so when it appears both infinite and perfect, that is to say, divine. The conditions required to render man conscious of a manifestation of the divine, vary according to the degree of development his mind may have attained. In the childhood of his race he bowed down before the phenomena and forces of Nature. When he reached greater maturity he heard God's voice in the moral law, and sought Him in the supreme reason of things. To the eyes of the Jewish people, when they had at last arrived at Monotheism, Nature revealed God, as the work discovers the workman; and religion, or the conscious union of the creature and the Creator, was found in the punctual observance of a moral and ritual law. While Polytheism was essentially a religion of nature, Judaism was in its essence a religion of law. Neither the one nor the other could be final. Jesus of Nazareth carried the religious consciousness an immense step forwards. He assumed this thought as the axiomatic basis of all his teaching, that the true relation of man to God is higher than the connection which unites even the most feeble with the Almighty on whom he depends, or subjects of law with their judge; and that this normal relation is one of affinity, and consequently of mutual love. Feeling in his inmost heart that God was the *Heavenly Father*, he thought it natural that all men should feel the same. The spirit of man is virtually one with the divine Spirit which moves and attracts it; such is the philosophical and religious principle of the gospel. God, therefore, is *our Father;* all men are by nature His children, and ought to live together in the consciousness of this divine parentage, and conformably to its obligations. Thus it was that, without setting aside either nature or law, Jesus introduced man into a kingdom higher than either, that of *grace*,—not in the arbitrary sense which theology has so often put upon this word, but in the natural sense of the sweet and strong attraction which the divine ideal exercises over the man to whom it is revealed. From this it follows, that love ought to be substituted for fear or calculation as the first motive-power of the religious and moral life. And hence, from this principle of a filial relation uniting man to God, spring the characteristic traits of the teaching of Jesus; hence the beautiful precepts of humanity, of compassion, brotherly love, tender sympathy for all those who suffer—for the poor, the sick, the oppressed; hence that assurance of the divine pardon in the soul which has recovered by repentance and the return to rectitude the guarantee of its divine destiny; hence the reiterated appeals to the free assent of conscience—for the human conscience, in virtue of the affinity between man and God, must intuitively recognize what is divine; hence that delight in life, and that frank participation in whatever enjoyments no higher duty forbids—for man ought to consider himself in this world as in one of the mansions of the Father's house, and nothing is less monachal than such a feeling;

hence, finally, the conditions with which Jesus connects real communion with God, conditions simply religious and moral, not in any way dogmatic or ritualistic, which may be summed up in purity of desire, in hunger and thirst after perfection, and in love to God. This is plainly his fundamental teaching. It appears, no doubt, under national forms and with accessory ideas belonging to his education and his time, but such ideas and forms cannot be properly included among the constituent elements of his doctrine. It would not be a mere play of words to affirm, that Jesus proclaimed at the same time the religion of humanity, and the humanity of religion.

But much would still be wanting to explain the propagating power possessed by this new ideal, if we confined ourselves to pointing out its abstract truth and beauty. Because a truth is proclaimed among mankind, it does not necessarily follow that it makes its way with the masses. Indeed the most elevated philosophical teaching never touches more than a few select minds. In vain would Jesus have expounded his sublime views upon the true relationship of man and God, if his person had not been itself the incarnation of the ideal which his teaching revealed to thought. He was himself quite aware of this, and, while admitting very plainly the possibility of a real communion with God outside the circle of his own personal influence, he recognized the fact that only those who attached themselves personally to him became thoroughly impregnated with his spirit. This kind of moral influence can no more be defined than can the attractive power of simple beauty. We feel, when we see Jesus, that in him appears the divine element which marks with its impress the revealers of the ideal; we say, *Ecce, ecce Deus!* But as to the philosophical or religious forms which shall embody this revelation of the divine, these depend upon the circumstances amidst which the revelation is made. It is probable that, if one like Jesus had appeared in Greece or Rome, the characteristics of this "something divine" would have been different from what they were in Galilee and Jerusalem. The attributes of a divine character are necessarily conceived in connection with the idea which is held as to what constitutes superiority in spiritual things. It was for this reason that, appearing as he did amongst the Jewish people, the first impression which Jesus made upon sympathizing souls was necessarily expressed in these words: "He is a prophet." And if this impression became such that those who felt it could conceive of nothing superior or even comparable to him who produced it, it could only break out in this exclamation: "It is the Messiah, he who was to come!" For a Jew could conceive of nothing higher upon earth.

This is in fact what took place. Jesus was at first to the people a prophet; afterwards, to his own followers, he was the Messiah or the Christ.*

---

* We know that Messiah is in Hebrew what Christ is in Greek, and that these two words mean the Anointed—that is, of God. The Messiah was the King expected by the Jewish people to establish on their behalf the reign of justice and truth.

But in what light did he regard himself? This is a more difficult question to solve than is generally supposed. In the first place, it is connected with a great critical problem, the thorough discussion of which would require a volume,—that, namely, of the historical value of the fourth Gospel, attributed to the Apostle John. This book, in fact, speaks throughout, and makes Jesus speak, as if from the very first he had claimed and received from his disciples the honours due to a being of superhuman origin, of transcendent nature, existent long before his appearance on earth, and only passing a short time here to return almost immediately to the super-physical region whence he came. Could this have been the authentic teaching of the Founder of Christianity? Apart from all dogmatic discussion, modern criticism is now unanimous in admitting that the discourses contained in the fourth Gospel can only be considered as free compositions, similar to those which Christians of all times of mystic disposition —for example, the author of *The Imitation*—have much delighted to compose, forgetting to ask themselves (so certainly did they believe that they spoke in his name) whether their adored Master would always have sanctioned all that their glowing affection made him say. Thus in the fourth Gospel there are discourses in which the Evangelist makes his own reflections at the end of the teachings which he has previously put into the mouth of Jesus, where it is impossible to distinguish the point at which the writer substitutes himself for the speaker whom he had before presented.* The much less carefully studied and more popular character of the Christ of the three first Gospels justifies us in preferring their testimony to that of the fourth Evangelist, whose work is obviously composed in the interest of a particular doctrine. He is but one, they are three; and criticism finds in their narratives documents still more ancient and numerous. But a very simple observation will justify the line we take in putting aside for a moment the so-called Gospel of John. Whoever may be the author, whatever may be the date of this book, we can only put its doctrine as to the person of Jesus in the place logically belonging to it in the history of Christian beliefs, and that place could not be the first in order of time. When we think that from the beginning the Church has constantly obeyed the desire ever more and more to glorify him from whom it sprang; when we see each Evangelist, every Christian writer, assign to Jesus the highest dignity that he believes it possible to attribute to him; we cannot admit that primitive Christianity began by adoring in his person the eternal Word, and only at some time afterwards came to see in him a man born miraculously, and even a son of man in the full meaning of the term. The converse is the only course conceivable.

This point cleared up, the question returns, How,

* See, for example, the conversation of Jesus with Nicodemus, John iii. 5—21.

according to the three first Gospels, did Jesus regard himself?

We remark in the first place that no word from his own lips makes allusion to any miraculous circumstances attending his birth. He regards himself as a child of Nazareth, not of Bethlehem;* he reproves the scribes for teaching, contrary to the very texts which they called to their aid, that the Messiah must necessarily be a descendant of David;† and he does not himself put forth the least claim to such a descent. Yet he did not always refuse the title of Messiah. He believed then that he had a right to it. But it is proved by the well-known incident of the confession of Peter‡ that he did not appropriate this title to himself at his own instance, and that, for some time, his most intimate disciples followed him without thinking of conferring it upon him. If the feeling that he was in fact the Messiah, after having long germinated inwardly in his mind, became at last a clear and settled conviction, Jesus did not therefore seek to impose this belief upon others. It is probable that the presentiment of the inevitable conflict which must needs occur between the idea of the Messiah as he conceived it,—and as, in harmony with the consciousness he had of his religious mission, he desired it to be,—and that of the Messiah as his nation conceived it, was the cause which led him to this prolonged

---

* Matt. xiii. 54; Luke iv. 24.

† Mark xii. 35.   ‡ Matt. xvi. 13—17

reserve. No doubt the same conflict of ideas had agitated his soul long before it was definitively decided for him. In a word, Jesus would have desired, without himself directly prompting it, to be declared Messiah by the popular will; he would have wished to be the accepted Messiah, because he knew that he was unlike the expected Messiah.

He always called himself, from first to last, the *Son of Man*. Did this mean what orthodoxy in later times (when greatly embarrassed with the effort to reconcile the declarations of Jesus respecting himself with its own dogmas) would have it to mean, that he indicated by that phrase his *human nature*, to distinguish it from his *divine nature*, to which was reserved the name of *Son of God?* Not a word of his own warrants us in attributing to him this strange idea, according to which he would have spoken and acted sometimes as God, sometimes as man, while still remaining one and the same person. Besides, it is forgotten, when such language is used, that in biblical phrase the name *Son of God* supposes nothing which decidedly separates those who bear it from all other created beings. Angels and men are so designated in both Testaments,* and if the expression *the Son of God* was employed in the time of Jesus as a term of pre-eminence, and to designate a specific person, it was simply synonymous with Messiah, or was rather perhaps one of

---

* Gen. vi. 2; Job i. 6, ii. 1; Ps. lxxxii. 6; Hos. i. 10, &c. Matt. v. 9; Luke vi. 35, xx. 36; Gal. iii. 26, &c.

the honorary titles of the Messiah.* In point of fact, Jesus, in the first three Gospels, always humbles himself profoundly before God. He is tempted, he prays, he suffers, he weeps, he refuses to be addressed as God, reserving this for the Father alone;† he declares that he is ignorant of things which God only knows;‡ he submits his own will, overcoming its resistance not without difficulty, to that of God.§ If he calls God *his* Heavenly Father, he proclaims at the same time that He is also the Father of us all. He never represented to his disciples that it was a duty to worship him.‖ In a word, he was completely innocent of the charge which has been sometimes brought against him, that he wished to make himself pass for a God come down to earth.¶ As to the

---

* Compare Mark xiv. 61; Luke xxii. 67, 70; and also Matt. xvi. 16; Mark viii. 29; Luke ix. 20.

† Mark x. 18. ‡ Mark xiii. 32. § Matt. xxvi. 36—44.

‖ The adoration of a divine being must not be confounded with the *proskynesis*, the homage rendered to him who was looked upon as King or Messiah; for example, Matt. ii. 2, xiv. 33.

¶ Of all the sayings attributed by the three first Evangelists to Jesus before his death, two only could give sanction to the thought that he attributed the name Son of God to himself in any metaphysical and exclusive sense. The first is in Mark xiii. 32, where the *Son* is placed above angels and men. But this expression, besides being not particularly orthodox, is wanting in just the parallel passages, and has all the appearance of having been the addition of a copyist more or less Arian. Several manuscripts omit it. The other is in the passage, Matt. xi. 27, Luke x. 22, which strangely breaks the thread of the discourse, and resembles a rhythmical ecclesiastical formula. The fundamental idea of this passage may be authentic. Jesus, at the moment when he speaks, is conscious of being known properly only to God who reads his heart, while he alone thoroughly

enemies whom he encountered, it is evident that, if Jesus had proclaimed himself God, they would not have failed to make such a pretension, which was an unheard-of blasphemy to Jewish ears, the ground and the constant subject of their accusations. Now, not a single discussion of this kind arose, and the two points on which Jesus was judged by the Sanhedrim were, first, a bold word which he had spoken about the temple; secondly, and above all, the fact of his having declared himself the Messiah.

It has been asserted, and with more show of reason, that this name, *Son of Man*, signified from the first the Messiah, in allusion to the passage in the apocalypse of Daniel, in which the prophet sees *one like a Son of Man coming on the clouds of heaven** to be invested by God with dominion over the world. This explanation, however, all things considered, could hardly be the true one. There is no question in the passage of *the* Son of Man, nor even of a personal Messiah, but of a being of human form, this form being no other than the symbol of the Jewish people, arriving in the last place at universal empire, after four great historical empires —the Assyrian, Chaldean, Medo-Persian and Greek—

---

knows God as the Father. To this idea, which was so perfectly natural in the circumstances amidst which he lived, a different turn has been given under the influence of a subsequent theology. But be this as it may, we must admit that two isolated and apparently doubtful sayings cannot militate against the letter and the spirit of a whole mass of concordant statements. * Dan. vii. 13.

respectively symbolized by different animals, have succeeded each other upon the earth. But, in our judgment, one decisive circumstance settles the question. If Jesus from the commencement had appropriated to himself the title of Messiah by simply calling himself the Son of Man, how could his friends have so long regarded him as merely a prophet; and what would there have been new and spontaneous in the first proclamation of his Messiahship which won for Simon Bar-Jonas his surname of honour (Matt. xvi. 13—20)?

It is evident, in my opinion, that we must seek for the meaning of a title like this in the natural, popular idea which it must have suggested to the people who heard it employed. The expression *Son of Man* was not new to the Jews. The Old Testament uses it many times, and, even in the passage cited from Daniel, it is simply synonymous with the term *man*, expressing more emphatically the nature of the being so designated.* Like several of the prophets, and with a didactic purpose easy to divine, Jesus attached importance to these appellations chosen by him to designate himself, or to designate his disciples in a characteristic manner. The *Son of Man* then signifies, in relation to his religious mission, one who only wishes to be, and to know, man in his relations with God; whose religion consequently requires for its basis of reality simply the human nature

---

* Num. xxiii. 19; Job xxv. 6; Ps. viii. 4, lxxx. 17, cxliv. 3, cxlvi. 3; Ezek. ii. 1, 3, 6, 8, iii. 1, 3, 10, iv. 1, v. 1, vi. 2, vii. 2, &c.

common to all, whose claim, at once humble and vast, is, to be the first to realize in his own person this strictly human religion. This is not saying that Jesus thus presents himself of set purpose, and in a manner little agreeable to modesty, as a type and model of humanity. It simply means that he has a consciousness of the true relation which ought to unite man to God, and that he has the just conception of a life in conformity with the principles derived from this essential relation.*

Hence it is only in a solemn and significant manner that Jesus employs this term. It is in the capacity of Son of Man, that is to say, in the name of the purely human religion of which he is the bearer and the medium, that he speaks with authority; that he condemns or pardons; that he interprets broadly the law of the Sabbath; that he says he has come to save and not to destroy, to minister, not to be ministered to; that he considers himself the head of that kingdom of God

---

* *Son of Man* rather than *man;* for in Hebrew the word *son*, besides its proper sense, expresses essential affinity, intimate connection, material or moral. The *sons of the prophets* are their disciples (2 Kings ii. 3; compare Matt. xii. 27); *sons of death* for *doomed to death* (Ps. cii. 20, lxxix. 11); *sons of flame* for *sparks* (Job. v. 7), &c. It has been said that the apocryphal apocalypse of Enoch, a little before the appearance of Jesus, already employs this name of Son of Man to designate the Messiah. A critical judgment, more acute in our opinion, distinguishes in this book the hands of two writers, the one anterior, the other posterior, to the Gospel. The Messiah is called *Son of Man* only by the latter. But again, nothing of this sort can put aside the fact that, according to our Gospels, the Jewish people of the time of Jesus were not at all accustomed thus to designate the Messiah; and this is all that need be insisted upon here.

which he desires to inaugurate, without concealing from himself the fact that the Son of Man knows not where to lay his head; that he accepts homage, and resigns himself to evil treatment. It is also in this capacity that he considers himself as having the perfect right to judge men in what relates to religion and morals. Nor must we forget that he maintains the distinction between attachment to his person, and communion with God. A man may be forgiven when he speaks against the Son of Man, but not when he speaks against the Holy Spirit; when he has wilfully become an enemy of the good, and a denier of the true.*

We are therefore justified in saying,—to state precisely in modern language the opinion that Jesus had of himself,—that he had the clear consciousness of a divine vocation, which impelled him to found the pure, human religion, the germs of which were contained in the law and the prophets of his people. Persuaded as he was that no work, no mission, could be higher than that, and that on it depended the future of his own nation and of the world, this consciousness identified itself in his mind with that of being the true Messiah, after whom it would be in vain to look for another.†

---

* Matt. xii. 31, 32.

† How evident this is in his answer to the messengers of John the Baptist when they are sent by their master to inquire if *it is he who is to come* (Matt. xi. 1, &c.)! Jesus, in fact, does not reply either yes or no, but it is clear that he would wish to see the Baptist rise to the idea that the true Messiahship is realized by him. It is with the same desire to give to the

Is it necessary to think besides this that he assigned to a future period the accomplishment of a miraculous and sudden renovation of the world, much more in accordance with the hopes of his countrymen than was the gradual transformation which he described in such wonderfully simple and impressive words—for example, in Mark iv. 26—29; Matt. xiii. 31—33? Or rather, in those passages of the Gospels which speak of his early return, of his glorious re-appearing, terrible to the wicked, but so blessed to the good, ought we not to see an alteration of his teaching made by his disciples, carried away by the desire to give to their own expectations the authority of a divine revelation? Or again, and this is our opinion, may there not have been in these fragments of the Gospels a commingling, which cannot now be parted, of poetical hopes and prophetic intuitions as to the radical revolution of which the world was to be the theatre, of which his work was the primary cause, and his person the prime mover,—may there not have been intuitions and hopes that Jesus often expressed under popular figures, without caring to distinguish the essence from the form of his previsions, and in such a manner that they might have been reported after his time by his followers in a sense still more in harmony with

popular Messianic ideas a bias which will bring them nearer his own, that he suggests to the people that they should behold in John the Baptist that Elias who, according to the scribes, was to prepare the way for the expected Messiah (Matt. xi. 14).

the Messianic expectations? The question is one of very great interest, but only indirectly relating to our subject.

The result of this first chapter, as regards our history, is, that Jesus, by the very consideration of the humanity to which he held so strongly, would clearly have repudiated every theory which attributed to him a superhuman origin; that the divine character of his human life made such an impression upon his disciples that they did not hesitate, and this with his own consent, to salute the Messiah in the Son of Man; and that, finally, enthusiastic attachment to his person, *faith in him*, was confounded in their minds with the adoption of his religion itself.

APPENDIX TO CHAPTER I.

ORTHODOX believers, and even the majority of unbelievers, generally appear so surprised when they hear the statement that Jesus had not the least intention to represent himself as God, that it may be needful to strengthen the foregoing direct exposition by indicating in what manner divines of the traditional school flatter themselves that they parry this blow, aimed straight at the heart of their system by historical criticism. We could not fix upon one among them more competent than the Abbé Troncy, who has taken upon himself the task of contesting almost all our assertions in the *Refutation* of which we have spoken in the Preface. If we do not altogether deceive ourselves, the result of this controversy is, that we are perfectly justified in affirming that Jesus never sought to inculcate upon his disciples the belief in his equality with God, and that, on the contrary, he always implied, and even directly taught, the opposite doctrine. It will be remembered that it is the narratives of the three first Gospels which form the basis of this discussion.

It is important to note in this place certain loyal admissions made by M. Troncy: "We admit," he says, pp. 33, 34, "that we do not find in the Synoptics (or the three first Gospels) the metaphysical theory of the Word, nor any affirmations so formal and explicit as St. John's respecting the divinity of Christ..... The name of God is not, it is true, applied to Jesus by the three first Evangelists; neither do we find in their books an express, formal declaration that he existed in eternity before his incarnation." But in all that they tell us of him, "the conviction is taken for granted that one who has a mission like his, who is invested with such power, who fulfils such functions, is a being whose nature is necessarily divine."

We must here make a preliminary remark, and one which, according to our view, is conclusive, with regard to a concession which will certainly astonish those who have not studied the question closely. What! The three first Evangelists take up their pens with the conviction **that Jesus is God, the sovereign Being who created the world,** and that he has become incarnate for the salvation of men—they believe that **adherence to this fundamental** truth of the Gospel **is of absolute necessity for the eternal** happiness of the soul; that on it depends the efficacy of the redemption, the value of Christianity, and our common hope; that to deny this, or even to be ignorant of it, **is to** have no share in the elementary conditions of salvation—they undertake accordingly the sacred work of making known to Jews and heathens who **have no** conception **of** him this Jesus-God in whom all must believe if they would be saved—they relate what they know of his life, of his teaching, of his disputations with malignant and cunning **adversaries**; they delight to make prominent his power, his sublimity, his titles to the reverence of the human race; and not once, **not in a** single instance, **is this** simple assertion, *Jesus is God*, this formal declaration of a belief which fills their souls, to be found **in** their three records, **which** so resemble **each** other, while yet so greatly differing! Certainly this is incredible—about as likely, indeed, as the supposition that three historians, enthusiastic admirers of the first Napoleon, could have written his life, always calling him General Buonaparte, without once mentioning his imperial title.

Nothing, moreover, could be more characteristic of the

Appendix to Chapter I.

school to which the Abbé Troncy belongs, than the attempt at explanation which he proposes (p. 95) in another very similar case. He suggests that it was "useless and even dangerous" to develop the doctrine of the incarnate Word before Jews and heathens; that it was necessary to take into account their state of mind, not to run counter too much to their prejudices, and thus to lead them on to "the supernatural persuasion of the faith." Here, then, we have our three Evangelists convicted of having acted as cunning tacticians—that is to say, of having jesuitically concealed the essence of their beliefs in order to beguile their readers. These humble and artless chroniclers, who were so happy to relate the wonders of their Master's life, are transformed into diplomatists. It is true that they did not scruple to give terrible offence to the Jews by maintaining that he who was crucified at Jerusalem was the Messiah of the national expectation, nor to expose themselves to the derision of the Greeks by pointing to the poor Rabbi of Nazareth as the revealer of the true religion. But their boldness extends no further, and they are prudently silent as to the eternal deity of the incarnate Son. It is in this way that the defenders of tradition understand history!

Not to delay longer over this subterfuge, which we can only regard as a piece of ecclesiastical trifling, let us see upon what ground the Abbé rests his assertion that, if the Jesus of the three first Gospels is silent as to his essential deity, he implies **it in** his teachings, in his acts, and in the claims which he puts forth.

First, **it is** upon this, that Jesus, in the Synoptics, assumes the attitude **of** a supreme legislator, of a reformer who fears not to change the law of God, who declares himself greater than the temple, and the superior of John the Baptist, whom nevertheless he pronounces the greatest among men. Nothing of all this denotes that Jesus is **God**. Paul, who set aside the Jewish law much more thoroughly than Jesus did, never on that account conceived himself to **be God**. He believed, **and Jesus believed also,** that the Jewish law, although divine in its origin, was imperfect and temporary, and that it must be either *fulfilled* (Jesus) or *abrogated* (Paul). Already rabbis like Hillel had sought for the essential, higher principle of the law before determining its sense, its application, and the relative importance **of its precepts** in detail. Several of the prophets had expressed themselves with great freedom upon certain legal prescriptions. Jesus went further under the inspiration of his religious genius, and with every justification, as we think, while even from the Jewish point of view he had entirely the right to do so **as a** prophet, much more as the **Messiah**. **Let us** add that Jesus did not say, though he might have said it, that he **was** "greater than the temple" (Matt. xii. 6), but that the gospel which he proclaimed was superior to the temple ($\mu\epsilon\hat{\imath}\zeta o\nu$ and not $\mu\epsilon i\zeta\omega\nu$, according to the Vatican, Cambridge, and Sinaitic manuscripts); and that he did not exalt himself above all men in proclaiming himself superior to John the Baptist, while declaring him the greatest of all; but that, in allusion to the lower degree of spirituality in which John the Baptist still remained, he said that "the least in the kingdom of heaven was greater than he" (Matt. xi. 11).

What again indirectly proves the deity of Jesus in the eyes of the Abbé is, that, according to the Synoptics, he wrought stupendous miracles, betokening an absolute power over nature, such miracles as God only could work. We shall not enter here into a discussion on the subject of miracles, which would involve us in a long digression. There are in these same Gospels certain passages which would limit the miraculous power of Jesus more than the Abbé seems to think (as Mark v. 8, vi. 5). But it will be sufficient to call to mind that the Bible relates a host of miracles at least as astonishing as those which are attributed to Jesus, without the conclusion having ever been thought of, that those who wrought them must have been incarnate deities.

But again, continues M. Troncy, it is proved by the fact that Jesus shows in the Gospels that he knows the secrets of the heart, that he forgives sins, that he proclaims himself to be the sovereign judge of men; all of which are pretensions that can belong only to God. I doubt whether Jesus knew from the beginning the secret heart of Judas. In any case, and even if we admit that we must recognize a supernatural faculty in a force of penetration which, according to our view, may have been very great without being superhuman, we should remember that in the primitive church the "discerning of spirits," or "of hearts," was considered a gift of the Holy Spirit (comp. Acts v. 1 et seqq.), and not a proof of the personal divinity of any one possessing it. As to the pardon of sins, Jesus pronounces it to those whom he sees sincerely penitent, by virtue of one of the essential principles of his religion, the Fatherhood of God, and not of his arbitrary will (Matt. vi. 12). He even intimates that this consolatory office may also be discharged by his true disciples (ibid. xviii. 18). Here is not the shadow of a pretension to be considered as a God. Finally, as to the last judgment, that was a function which, according to Jewish ideas, belonged of right to the Messiah (comp. Matt. iii. 12, xix. 28).

But the Abbé Troncy also specifies, as so many indirect indications of the divinity of Jesus Christ, that he promises eternal life to his faithful disciples—which, however, naturally follows from the persuasion he felt that his religion realized the normal and true relation between man and God; that he presents himself as a "propitiatory offering" for sin—a fact which appears to us a very doubtful matter, but which historically implies nothing indicative of his divinity; and that, in his discourses to the disciples after his resurrection, he promises to be with his church even to the consummation of all things. We may be allowed to refrain from discussing in a *history* the words attributed to Jesus after his death; but, in any case, nothing in such a declaration goes beyond the idea of a being who now belongs to the heavenly state, but remains united by his spirit to those who continue faithful to him. Besides, we have no intention of disputing the place which Jesus claims in the memory, the affection, the confidence of his followers: this very legitimate claim has nothing to do with the question before us. Above all, we must not forget that Jesus himself allows, as we have seen, that it is possible to have a place in the kingdom of heaven apart from his own direct and personal influence.

We have now gone through the formal proofs that were promised us, to counterbalance the ominous silence of Jesus himself, and of the three first Evangelists, upon his essential deity. We leave our readers to judge of their value. But there are still some points raised by M. Troncy which it will be well to elucidate.

He has not been able to dispute the fact that the title *Son of God* is very often given in the Bible to created beings, men or angels. But he affirms that Jesus receives or assumes it in an ontological, exclusive sense (which ought to have been proved, but is not), and that this expression, applied pre-eminently to an individual, is not, in the same books, one of the synonyms, or one of the honorary titles, of the Messiah. It seems to us, however, impossible not to yield to the evidence which is presented by the comparison of three parallel passages relating to the same event, that of the first acknowledgment of the Messianic dignity of Jesus by the Apostle Peter:

MATT. xvi. 16:	MARK viii. 29:	LUKE ix. 20:
"Simon Peter answered: Thou art the Christ, the Son of the living God."	"Peter answered him: Thou art the Christ."	"Peter answered: Thou art the Christ of God."

So also in the examination before the High-priest Caiaphas:

MATT. xxvi. 63:	MARK xiv. 61:	LUKE xxii. 67, 70:
"I adjure thee by the living God, that thou tell us whether thou be the Christ, the Son of God."	"Art thou the Christ, the Son of the blessed?"	"Art thou the Christ? Tell us." Jesus answers, affirming his Messiahship. "Art thou then the Son of God?"

It is clear that, if this expression had been equivalent to the name of *God*, the enemies as well as the friends of Jesus—the former in order to mark what would have been in their eyes a fearful blasphemy, the latter in order to render a perfect homage to their Master—would not have failed to bring out such a signification. The latter especially would have carefully guarded themselves against giving this name to men, as they do, Matt. v. 9; Luke xx. 36.

Appendix to Chapter I.

As regards the name *Son of Man*, the only name, we repeat, which Jesus himself assumes, the Abbé Troncy, agreeing in this with all orthodox tradition, unhesitatingly refers it to the human nature of the incarnate God, so that the *Son of Man* would signify Jesus-man, and the *Son of God* Jesus-God; and he altogether questions the sense which we have given to this expression as connecting it with the work which Jesus sought to perform as prophet and Messiah. He considers this designation, understood as a synonym for *man*, to be without meaning, since no person living needs inform his fellow-creatures that he is a man. Jesus, he says, would not have taken such a name if he had not possessed another, loftier one, which determines its dogmatic value. In thus reasoning the Abbé forgets several things: 1st, the name *Son of Man*, taken in the sense in which we understand it, is only apparently without meaning, and it is its paradoxical look at first sight which leads to reflection upon the motives which determined the choice of it; 2nd, by the hypothesis preferred by the Abbé, this name signifies *man* quite as much as in ours; only he would determine the force of it by comparison with the superhuman nature which he attributes to Jesus, while we believe that this may be found in the strictly human character of the principles of religion which he has implanted in humanity; 3rd, it is precisely in his capacity as *Son of Man* (quite logically according to our explanation, very heretically in that of M. Troncy) that Jesus exercises those functions, claims those rights, and puts forth those pretensions, which, according to our opponent, presuppose his divine nature,—the forgiveness of sins (Matt. ix. 6), the reform of the law of the Sabbath (ibid. xii. 8), the last judgment (ibid. xxv. 31), &c.; 4th, the only system in which it would have been inadmissible for Jesus so to style himself is, if we except Gnosticism, that of orthodox tradition; for, that he should have been able to call himself the *Son of Man*, he must have had in strict consistency a human father, which is precisely what, according to orthodoxy, Jesus had not. Could it have been the fear of venturing on this dangerous ground that deterred the Abbé from attempting any explanation of the two genealogies, which both agree in giving to Jesus a human father, Joseph, the husband of Mary?

In conclusion, the Abbé Troncy, like all of his school, would explain the imperfections, the limitations, the temptations, the sufferings, and the death of Christ, by referring them simply to the human nature of Jesus, distinct from his divine nature; doubtless forgetting that he had before found an indication of his divinity in the propitiatory passion. For example, when Jesus in his agony prays to God, saying, *Not my will, but thine be done*, we are to understand that it is as a man that he prays thus, while he knows very well that as God he has no other will than that of God himself, and that in fact he is praying to himself. Again, when Jesus rebukes the rich young man for thoughtlessly applying to him the epithet *good*, which could only be strictly applied to the all-perfect Being, it is as if he said to him: If thou knewest to whom thou art speaking, I should not blame thee; but, as thou knowest him not, I rebuke thee for having spoken the truth without being aware of it. In the same way, when it is related in that admirable but strange myth of the temptation in the wilderness, that the devil carries Jesus away and places him successively upon the roof of the temple and upon a mountain, it behoves us to think that, while in truth there is only one person in the God-man, yet here it is the man alone who is carried away and tempted, since it would be utterly impossible to conceive that the Creator was for a single moment, even in imagination, transported by Satan through the air. But what then becomes of the unity of the person?

We pause here, because the applications of the famous distinction of natures too readily become grotesque, and therefore unfit to dwell upon. But the fault is not ours; it belongs to the orthodox theory, which resolves at any cost to attribute two natures, different, and in many respects irreconcilable, to one and the same personal being; whence it follows in fact that the same *ego*, the same person, is at the same instant tempted and incapable of being tempted, suffering and impassible, feeble and omnipotent, in subjection to God and equal with God, living and yet dead, &c. Are there not here enough of monstrous contradictions?

Let us remark, however, before concluding, the desperate efforts which the orthodox school have made to escape from the declaration of Jesus (Mark xiii. 32), that he is ignorant of the day and hour of the last judgment, which are known to the Father alone. **Note** that this declaration excludes from **this** knowledge *the Son*, whatever be the meaning we attach to that word. Bossuet reflected upon the expression "with trembling," which does not surprise us when we see him employing his magnificence of style to expound it thus, after endless oratorical precautions: "I have foretold to you all that was necessary for you to **know. If I** say, **in** order to keep you within these limits, that **I know** no more, I have my reasons for so speaking, in accordance with the charge imposed upon me, the part that I am called upon to take" (*Méditations sur l'Evangile*).

The Abbé Troncy piously accepts and reproduces Bossuet's explanation, which, we must say, shocks and wounds us. This Jesus, who "has his reasons" for speaking the contrary of the truth, who "acts a part," is even less edifying than the prudent Evangelists keeping silence **on the** divinity of Christ from diplomatic motives.

We venture to regard our line of thought as rendered more secure by its refutation, and are glad to leave these church subtilties, to return to the domain of natural and self-consistent history, which, instead of obscuring the patent facts, seeks to clear **up** what is obscure, and to bring anew to life, not phantoms, but realities.

CHAPTER II.

THE FIRST DISCIPLES OF JESUS.

An ardent, impassioned love of Jesus was the first motive-power of the history we are now to continue. The disciples forgot the distinction maintained by the Master between the pure religion which he taught and exemplified, and faith in his person. Jesus himself, and not the religious realities which Jesus had revealed to the consciousness, became the object, properly speaking, of the religious belief. There was consequently a natural tendency increasingly to exalt his person.

During his earthly life, the enthusiasm of his disciples had already woven for him the Messianic crown. After his death, the craving to glorify him was still more intense. Like a ship on tropical seas thrown into relief by the dazzling brilliancy of its own track, Jesus crucified appeared to his followers in that state of celestial transfiguration which had so impressed some of them, though but for a moment, during the days of his flesh.*
The faith in his corporeal resurrection, the determining occasion of which was the obscure fact of the empty tomb, had its real and profound cause in the ineffaceable impression which his religious grandeur had left on the

---

* Mark ix. 2—8, and parallel passages. The close analogy between the scene of the transfiguration and the visions of the risen body is not sufficiently noted.

minds of his faithful followers. A sound philosophy must admit that the higher manifestations of the spiritual life make the heart feel that the human personality is immortal. It is in this sense that we conceive the sentiment to have been a correct one which inspired in the first disciples the belief in the continued existence of their Master. But in the irreconcilable statements which have come down to us respecting the appearances of the risen one, we can see nothing more than the reflection of touching and poetical ecstacies, in which hearts burning with love, in strong reaction from their momentary depression, represented to themselves this survival under the form, at once material and ideal, which their Jewish training suggested to their excited imaginations. "I am he that was dead, but am alive for evermore;"* such for them, whenever they beheld its appearance, was the declaration of that august form on which their life henceforth depended.

Thus it was that in their thought the Messiah, unacknowledged while living, but victorious in death, "seated at the right hand of God," that is, having received from God all power in heaven and on earth,† and being destined soon to return to reign with his followers over a regenerated world, did not indeed cause to be forgotten, but nevertheless most often filled the place of, the humble Son of Man, misunderstood and persecuted. This modification of their views which was adopted by the first

* Rev. i. 18. † Matt. xxviii. 18.

Christians did not as yet separate Jesus from humanity. One who has been seen eating, sleeping, and suffering, cannot be taken so far out of the sphere of tangible realities. But it was natural that, preferring to glance forward to the future rather than to plunge again into a sad past, they should more readily contemplate their Master under this form of *man become celestial* than under that of the Rabbi of Nazareth. Though not yet deification, it was the beginning of an apotheosis.

We may clearly see this view maintained in the Apocalypse. That book, now no longer unintelligible, with its glowing symbolism, and strong colouring of images and descriptions, expressly ascribes the divine attributes to the glorified Jesus.* He is, like God, the first and the last, the Alpha and the Omega.† He bears upon his forehead a *new* name, which is none other than the ineffable name of Jehovah.‡ He is called the *Word of God*.§ But here let us not deceive ourselves. The author of the Apocalypse only means by this that Jesus, victorious over the world and sin, has *gained* all these titles. They have been conferred upon him from without, as a reward of his victory. He is not therefore the less a created being.|| It is from a certain moment, it is after his death upon the cross, that the divine perfections have been adjudged to him.¶ The name of God,

---

* Rev. i. 8, iv. 8. † Ibid. i. 11, 17, ii. 8, xxii. 13.
‡ Ibid. ii. 17, xix. 12. § Ibid. xix. 13.
|| Ibid. iii. 14. ¶ Ibid. v. 6 et seqq.

inscribed upon his forehead, will **one day** be written upon the foreheads of the elect.* His name, "Word of God," signifies that he is the revealer of the truth, the announcer of the divine judgments; and it is very far from bearing the metaphysical signification of the "Logos," or the "Word" in the sense of Philo.† The author considers Jesus as the offspring of the nation of Israel, the woman and mother of chapter xii., whose head is encircled by twelve stars (the twelve tribes). He is therefore the glory of his people, because it is from their race that he derives his birth; and nothing could be more contrary to all these ideas than the supposition of a supernatural origin, without ordinary human generation. The Apocalypse, which was written during the few months following the death of Nero (the beast whose number is indicated, xiii. 18),‡ dates from the year 68 of our era; but, excepting in the occasionally vehement exaggeration of its expectations, it adheres to the very earliest forms of the Christian belief.

If we return to the three first Gospels, not asking as before what witness Jesus gave to himself, but in order to learn what his historians thought of him, we shall find there the feeling still very strong that Jesus positively belongs to humanity; and if of evangelical documents we only possessed the Gospel of Mark

---

* Rev. ii. 17. † Comp. i. 9, xix. 9.

‡ It is now known that the number 666 is equivalent to the sum of the Hebrew letters which form the name *Cæsar Nero*.

and the discourses of the Apostles in the Acts, the whole Christology of the New Testament would be reduced to this: that Jesus of Nazareth was "a prophet mighty in deeds and in words, made by God Christ and Lord."* There would even be no reason to question the favourite dogma of the old Ebionites, the orthodox of the primitive times of whom we shall have to speak again, according to whose opinion Jesus had himself no consciousness of his vocation until the period of his baptism in the Jordan, when the heavens were opened and the Holy Spirit descended upon him. "A holy man, fully inspired by the divine spirit," would therefore have been the prescribed Christological formula.

With regard to the Gospels of Matthew and Luke, the two genealogies which these books respectively set forth plainly and expressly prove the strength of the primitive belief that Jesus was really man by his nature and birth. The object of these genealogies was to show that Jesus was truly the Messiah, by giving the list of his ancestors in direct line from King David to Joseph, the husband of Mary. This very appellation of *Son of David* was, indeed, one of the titles of the Messiah referred to in some passages from the prophets. Jesus sometimes received this title of honour from those who were asking a favour of him, or who desired to exalt his person, but we do not find that he ever assumed it himself. Nay,

---

* Mark i. 1—12; Acts ii. 22, 30, 36, iii. 22, 23, x. 38; comp. Luke xxiv. 19.

more—there is in the Gospel of Mark a very singular passage, in which, while disputing with the scribes, Jesus sets himself to show that they were deceived in their idea that the Messiah must necessarily be a descendant of David.* In any case, it is certain that the authors of the two genealogies regarded Jesus, as did his countrymen and contemporaries, as the eldest son of Joseph, the husband of Mary, and had not the least idea of a miraculous conception. If they had really had this idea, they would have presented the genealogy of Mary, and not that of Joseph. All the artifices used by the old commentators to reconcile this inconsistency of the evangelical narratives are shattered against the resistance of the texts. The divergences of the two genealogies simply prove that, even if the idea of the descent of Jesus from David was widely spread at an early period in Christian circles,† his family had not succeeded in settling the roll of his ancestors. In various ways, therefore, could the endeavour be made to connect him with the royal family of Israel. The most natural supposition was the one first started, for which we have the authority of our first Gospel, namely, that Joseph, the father of Jesus, was descended from David by Solomon and the line of the kings of Judah, their direct successors. But

* Mark xii. 35—37.

† This idea appears to have been already admitted in the time of St. Paul, Rom. i. 3. From the belief that Jesus was the Messiah, men passed to the belief that he was descended from David, but not from the latter to the former.

whether on account of historical difficulties, or rather from a repugnance to reckoning among ancestors of the Messiah idolatrous or wicked princes, of whom a large number appear in this long lineage, others preferred what may be called a younger branch, descending from David by Nathan. It is not our present object to inquire which were right and which wrong, nor even whether any were in the right. It suffices for our purpose to prove that, in the mind of the two genealogists, Jesus is the son of Joseph, born, like ourselves, of a man and a woman. Such was the persuasion of all his contemporaries, especially of the inhabitants of Nazareth, who were well acquainted, as they said, with his father, his mother, and his brothers.*

It is, then, very surprising that the same Gospels which have registered these genealogies, should be precisely those which have accredited in the Church the idea of the miraculous birth of Jesus. In the first Gospel the two contradictory notions are placed in abrupt juxtaposition, as though its compiler had not even perceived their incompatibility. The third is decidedly sensible of the contradiction,† and yet he compiles his history as if it did not exist. It is probable that the two Evangelists, considering the paucity of the traditions which were in circulation respecting the infancy of Jesus, did not venture to omit any of those which came to their knowledge, but put together the little

* Luke iv. 22; Mark vi. 3; Matt. xiii. 35. † Luke iii. 23.

they had gathered on this obscure subject, one on which Jesus himself had never spoken. Is it not evident, for instance, that when Luke relates how Joseph and Mary understood nothing of their son's words when, at twelve years of age, he told them that he must above all things be about his Father's business,* he is recording a tradition formed amongst people who knew nothing of the miraculous scenes which, according to the same Evangelist, had attended his birth, and the significance of which Mary, at least, could not have altogether mistaken?

Whence, then, arose this idea of a miraculous conception of Jesus in the womb of Mary? If his birth had been illegitimate, a suspicion which was in fact suggested in later times by the opponents of Christianity, his personal enemies in Galilee, and especially at Nazareth, where he was looked upon with less admiration, where he was less loved than elsewhere, would not have failed to reproach him with it, and we should certainly have found some trace of the fact in the accounts of his life. On the other hand, neither Mark, Paul, John, nor any other New Testament writer, speaks of the miraculous conception. Let us not be charged with inferring too much from the silence they maintain on this point. Such a belief, once adopted, is one of those which, even in the absence of a direct affirmation, make their presence felt in all kinds of latent modes. It does

* Luke ii. 42—50.

not then belong to the earliest phase of the Christian faith, and it is the first attempt to separate Jesus from humanity with the intention of glorifying him. Not that this miraculous conception was proposed with the view of saving Jesus from the stain of original sin. The early Christians had no idea of a fall of the human species, or of a hereditary taint propagated by generation. The belief that Jesus was miraculously conceived by the Holy Spirit must have been formed by the combination of two elements, which may be represented thus:— First, the idea that Jesus had been inspired by the Holy Spirit only from the time of his baptism in the Jordan, whilst previously he was not distinguished from the rest of mankind, had the defect of supposing, against all probability, the total, sudden, mechanical transformation of an ordinary man into a man without peer. On this supposition, it was the Holy Spirit, and no longer Jesus himself, who was the agent, properly so-called, in the salvation of men. That the baptism in the Jordan marked a crisis in the inner life of Jesus, in which a flash of light from above, illuminating his soul, completely revealed him to himself, is very possible; and it is even difficult to understand, excepting in some such view, the very great importance of this baptism in the eyes of the Evangelists and of the Jew-Christian party. But evidently Jesus must have previously given many proofs of his religious genius, and what we infer from psychological probability, the desire to glorify his person also suggested. It became a settled conviction that Jesus had been "filled with the Holy Spirit" from his youth, from his childhood, "from his mother's womb." In the religious phraseology of the Jews, this last expression was often employed to indicate that a good or evil quality appears as far back as possible in the past life of any person—was, so to speak, born with him. Thus Job calls himself the protector of the widow and the orphan from his mother's womb, and the Psalmist declares himself to have been a sinner at the moment of his birth.*

In the second place, the Hebrew nation, like many others, inclined to the belief that its great heroes had not come into the world in the ordinary manner. Already in the births of Isaac, Samson, and Samuel, there had been something of the miraculous. The same idea gained credence with respect to John the Baptist, who was also born in a manner contrary to all probability, and who from his mother's womb was filled with the Holy Spirit.† This idea was certainly applied to Jesus by his disciples. But could one rest there, and only attribute to Christ a prerogative shared by others? No. Superior to all who had *received* the Holy Spirit from the earliest age, he must have been *conceived* by the Holy Spirit; and this word, which so energetically expressed the absolute character of his divine inspiration, would readily become incorporated in a narrative which materialized it in a

* Job xxxi. 18; Ps. li. 5.   † Luke i. 15.

certain manner by the exclusion of the human father. The interpretation we give to this particular form of the earliest Christian legend is so congenial to the spirit and methods of the time, that, in that section of Christendom in which Jesus was still regarded as a son of Joseph, they made of the Holy Spirit—a feminine noun in Hebrew—not the begetter, but the *mother* of Jesus. Ἡ μήτηρ μοῦ τό ἅγιον πνεῦμα, *my mother the Holy Spirit*, says Jesus in the Gospel of the Hebrews.*

This doctrine of the miraculous conception glorified the person of Jesus, but at the expense of his personal superiority. If the greatness of Jesus consists in his religious and moral perfection, it is evidently on the condition that he has triumphed over the propensities inherent to human nature. If, on the contrary, a miraculous origin is attributed to him, what is there left to admire in virtues which cost him nothing? But those who inculcated this belief on the Church did not look at the matter so closely. Jesus was for them not the less a man, but only a man born miraculously.† No thought either of pre-existence or of incarnation was associated in their minds with this mystical dogma. The fact is, that the two ideas cannot be reconciled. A pre-existent being who becomes man, reduces himself,

---

* Cited by Origen, *Homil. in Jerem.* xv.

† That was thought sufficient, however, to justify the application to Jesus of the title *Son* [of God, being understood] in an absolute sense, as Matt. xi. 27, xxviii. 19.

if you will, to the state of a human embryo; but he is not *conceived* by action exterior to himself in the womb of a woman. Conception is the point at which an individual is formed who did not exist before, at least as an individual. On the contrary, where the question arises of a pre-existence or an incarnation,—in the writings, for instance, of Paul and John, nothing is said of a miraculous conception.

The three first Gospels, according to the approximate date assigned to them, may be regarded as the witnesses to the belief of the Church at the close of the first century and the beginning of the second. Earlier, however, but outside the circles that furnished the documents and traditions made use of by their compilers, a most original Christian doctrine had already begun in another way to elevate Jesus above humanity, though without severing all tie of original connection between them. I speak of Paul and his peculiar theology.

The great merit of Paul consists in this, that he emancipated the Church from the trammels of Jewish ritualism, and substituted for the observance of an outward law the inward principle of faith as the source and foundation of the religious life. In this point he is faithful to the inmost thought of Jesus. His fault was, perhaps, that he gave to the person of Jesus, as the object of faith, an importance so absolute, so exclusive, that Christianity, instead of remaining the faith *of* Jesus Christ became with him decidedly faith *in* Jesus Christ.

It is not then surprising that the Christ whom he offered to faith was more emphatically the "celestial man" who had been seen to appear to his first disciples after his cruel death, and whom Paul also saw revealing himself to him in his glory in the famous vision on the way to Damascus. Paul, besides, had not like them followed the earthly footsteps of him whom he preached with all the fire and mysticism of his ardent soul. It even appears, at least if we may judge by his Epistles, that he had no delight in dwelling upon those events in the life of Jesus which were unconnected with the history of the passion and the resurrection. Did he fear that, in going further back, he should subordinate himself too much to a tradition which his colleagues and rivals in the apostleship alone possessed at first hand? He evidently puts a certain emphasis on the declaration that he wishes to know only the Christ according to the spirit.* The Christ according to the spirit is properly the *man become celestial* of the Apocalypse and the first Gospels, but the word *become* disappears, and he remains the *man from heaven*,† a man apart, superior to all other men, having, no doubt, a common origin with humanity difficult to define, but nevertheless a man whose existence prior to his advent upon earth is taught with increasing clearness in proportion as the Pauline theology develops itself in the Epistles bearing the name of the Apostle of the Gentiles.

* 2 Cor. v. 16. † 1 Cor. xv. 47.

Here we are anew confronted with a problem which complicates our inquiry. To say nothing of the Epistle to the Hebrews, which most certainly is the production of another writer, are all the Epistles attributed to Paul authentic? Not only do the contents of what are called the Pastoral Epistles, that is the letters to Timothy and Titus, suggest in our opinion strong doubts on this point, but further, some very eminent critics have only recognized those addressed to the Romans, the Corinthians, and the Galatians, as proceeding directly from St. Paul. And one of their principal arguments is drawn from the unquestionable fact that the Christology of the other Epistles differs markedly from that of these four. While in them is not as yet taught, according to Dr. Baur, the pre-existence of Jesus, the Epistles to the Philippians, Ephesians, and Colossians teach it expressly, and would even make the supernatural being who lived for a time among men under the name of Jesus, the foundation and former of the whole creation.

We cannot here enter upon the discussion of these difficult questions, nor will it be necessary, if we speak of a Pauline Christology rather than of a Christology of Paul. If all the Epistles are authentic, they would show that Paul's ideas respecting the person of Jesus were developed with time; if they are only partly so, it was at any rate in his school that the Christology received this development, and it is certain that the undisputed Epistles lay down principles from which the doctrine of the disputed Epistles is frequently only the deduction. We must not, however, expect here very clear and self-consistent definitions. The Pauline Christology is a transition, and consequently contains elements which cannot always be reconciled. Sometimes Christ is positively man,* sometimes he seems to have scarcely anything in common with man, and his body, his flesh, bears only a "resemblance" to ours.† In one place we find the old Christian idea that he gained a name above every other name by the sufferings which he voluntarily bore for the good of men.‡ In another he was already so exalted many ages before he came upon earth, that we cannot conceive how he could rise still higher, unless he became equal with God,§ which the Pauline doctrine would not allow. However sublime may be, in fact, the position which it assigns to Jesus in the order of beings, this doctrine maintains the inferiority of Jesus before God, and never goes beyond the purport of the definition which it gives of him, Coloss. i. 15, as "*the first-born of the* whole creation" ($\pi\rho\omega\tau\acute{o}\tau o\kappa o\varsigma\ \pi\acute{a}\sigma\eta\varsigma\ \kappa\tau\acute{\iota}\sigma\epsilon\omega\varsigma$).‖

---

* Rom. i. 3, v. 15; 1 Tim. ii. 5; 1 Cor. xv. 21.
† Rom. viii. 3.   ‡ Philipp. ii. 6—11.   § 1 Cor. viii. 6.
‖ And not *the firstborn before the whole creation*, as the Abbé Troncy translates it, in which case it would have been $\pi\rho\grave{o}\ \pi\acute{a}\sigma\eta\varsigma\ \kappa\tau\acute{\iota}\sigma\epsilon\omega\varsigma$. Comp. 1 Cor. iii. 22, xi. 3, xv. 27, and seqq. &c. Nor should the passage in Rom. ix. 5 be adduced as proof to the contrary, which can only be translated as it is in the common version by means of a wrong punctuation, and really terminates with the customary doxology, *God who is above all be blessed for evermore*. Otherwise we must admit that Paul identifies the Christ

And here it is particularly to be regretted that we have no positive information upon the rabbinical doctrine from which the disciple of Gamaliel borrowed the elements of his transcendent conception of things. Might not what seemed to his mind a *pre-existence*, have been simply what we should denominate *pre-eminence*? In a curious book, entitled, *Jahrhundert des Heils* (*The Century of Salvation*), M. Gfrörer has shewn that the ancient rabbis often identified the two ideas, or rather substituted the one for the other. For example, in several rabbinical treatises the law, and the name of the Messiah, are represented as anterior to the world. It is easy to distinguish the speculative idea which is expressed under this form. In God, as in all intelligent being, that which stands pre-eminently in view in every process of development as its object, and consequently its final cause, *exists before* ideally in all the intermediate terms, which must nevertheless precede its real appearance. Jesus once considered as the culminating point of humanity, and humanity as that of the world, an ideal pre-existence anterior to the world must in this view be attributed to him. The manner in which Paul, in his undisputed Epistles, establishes his favourite parallelism of the two Adams,* the first and the last; the one earthly and

according to the flesh with the Eternal, which is inadmissible from any point of view, and above all from his. Neither should be cited 1 Tim. iii. 16, *God manifest in the flesh*, in place of **God** *manifested:* the most ancient manuscripts have simply *he who was manifested.*

* Rom. v. 12—21; 1 Cor. xv. 21, 22, 45—49.

physical, the other heavenly and spiritual; the one the principle of sin and death for the whole race, the other the principle of holiness and life, as if the sort of polary opposition existing in every man between the flesh and the spirit were repeated in the metaphysical region in which collective humanity forms but a single being,*— all this kind of conception belongs properly to rabbinical speculations, no doubt less subtile, but yet nearly allied with those which afterwards, in the system of the Cabbala, assumed the existence of the Adam Kadmon.

Strictly speaking, the Pauline theology does not as yet separate the person of Jesus from humanity, although his community of nature with it is no further preserved than by an obscure bond of connection, continually growing smaller. The various elements of this Christology may be brought together and recapitulated thus: Jesus is essentially spirit,† the man from heaven,‡ the subordinate creator of the world,§ possessed already of divine prerogatives before his coming upon earth, but having gained a still higher degree of heavenly dignity because, instead of making a selfish use of this "form of God," instead of proudly laying claim to equality with God, he

---

* Paul believed that he was living at the end of all things, and in his speculative theories he readily takes humanity as an organic whole, whose destiny and internal contradictions are decreed from on high. See, for example, Rom. xi. 32. Jesus is the spirit of humanity, of which Adam is the body. † Rom. i. 3.

‡ 1 Tim. ii. 5; 1 Cor. xv. 45—49. § Coloss. i. 16; 1 Cor. viii. 6.

voluntarily humbled himself to the lowest ranks of humanity, even to the "form of a slave," and to the death of the cross.* This "form of God," indeed (contrary to the orthodox interpretation), must be something else than equality with God, since he who possessed it has received, as a reward for his self-renunciation, a title and privileges superior to those he had before. At the same time, on account of the identity in essence and origin of his humanity and ours, both seeming to proceed from one and the same act of creative power, Jesus is the firstborn among many brethren,† and we ought to reproduce in ourselves his image,‡ and to grow until we have attained to his stature.§ Humanity in him, its head, the representative in whom it is spiritually comprehended, has appeased the divine wrath kindled by men's sins.‖ There is in each of us an inner, spiritual man, a *Christ in us*, which ought to rise to the height of its heavenly prototype.¶ If the "fulness of the Godhead" (the plentitude of perfection) dwelt "bodily" in him, it was that we might be filled with it ourselves;** and when all men, regenerated by his spirit, shall have become like him, then, his actual superiority over them no longer existing, his kingdom will, by that fact itself, come to an end, and God will be all in all men, as now he is all in

---

* Philipp. ii. 6—11. † Rom. viii. 29. ‡ Ibid.
§ Eph. iv. 13. ‖ Rom. iii. 23—26.
¶ Rom. viii. 10; 2 Cor. xiii. 5; Eph. iv. 13. ** Coloss. ii. 9, 10.

him.* Later orthodoxy has never been able to evade the strict meaning of this last passage excepting by subtile reasonings which do not deserve discussion. All these assertions, we must confess, are not perfectly coherent, and they leave room for many unsolved questions. In particular, we do not know how the Pauline Christology represented the entrance of its "man from heaven" into earthly humanity, in the line of David, whose descendant Paul believed him to have been *according to the flesh*. It keeps a profound silence, as we have said, upon the miraculous conception, which, besides, does not enter into the logical framework of such a system. The idea that Jesus is essentially man still forms a necessary part of it, and in this sense there is as yet no rupture with the primitive Christian view. But one cannot but perceive that this humanity of the Christ tends to disappear in the regions of speculative abstraction. In the later Epistles especially, Christ, who is henceforward called *the Son* in a transcendent sense, becomes more and more a mediating principle of the universe, or the point of solution of the metaphysical and moral contradictions of the world and of humanity.†

The Epistle to the Hebrews teaches a very similar Christology. Jesus is there described as superior to the angels; as, under God, the creator of the world; and as having attained, by his participation in the sorrows of humanity, to a still higher degree of glory and power.

---

* 1 Cor. xv. 28.   † Eph. i. 10.

The subordination of the Son to the Father is distinctly stated: but evidently the tendency henceforth is to reduce to a *minimum* the difference which distinguishes the Father from the Son, and we enter upon a new period in the development of the Christian belief.

CHAPTER III.

THE DOCTRINE OF THE WORD.

PAUL was little understood, and still less followed, during his lifetime. Many indications prove that his memory quickly fell into partial oblivion, if it was not even regarded with suspicion. The Jew-Christian view, which made it a necessary condition of salvation to observe the law in conjunction with faith in Jesus as the Messiah, became predominant in the very midst of the communities founded by Paul. It was not until the Jew-Christian Church, through the concurrent influence of events and of ideas tending constantly to soften the rigour of Jewish ritualism, was led to take up a practical ground very similar in fact to that which Paul would have desired it to occupy from the first, that he obtained the credit which inalienably belonged to him as the founder of the most distinguished Christian societies of the heathen world, and his writings became once more popular. Still, although tradition perpetuated his name among the great heroes of primitive Christianity, this was only done by placing him second to Peter, his rival and opponent, the Jewish Apostle who had remained faithful to the Jewish law.

It is not surprising, then, that, up to about the middle of the second century, Christological doctrine remained in a very undecided state. Documents relating to the first half of this century are scarce and fragmentary. Very few are of certain authenticity. Besides, it is easy to see that the principal interest of Christian writers was not yet directed, as was the case later, to the nature of Christ. Other subjects, such as monotheism, the future life, the new morality, the approaching end of the world, occupied them above all else; and the vagueness of the expressions employed respecting the person of Jesus plainly shows that on this point nothing was as yet determined in the views of the majority of Christians.

Nevertheless, it will be observed that in these views the "celestial being" increasingly supplanted the human being, except among the Jew-Christians of the primitive type, grouped together in Palestine and the region beyond the Jordan. These firmly maintained the opinion that Jesus was a man, the son of Joseph and Mary, fully inspired by God. A section of them, however, admitted his miraculous conception. There were some even who saw in him an angel descended from heaven, who had assumed a human body. *The Apostolic Fathers** broached opinions which were very little in accordance with each other. Barnabas sees in Jesus the being to whom God said, "Let us make man in our image" (ch. v.), who inspired the prophets and clothed himself in human flesh, that men might look upon him without being dazzled by his divinity. In the first Epistle attributed to Clement of Rome, there is nothing either original or clear, nor anything which cannot be reconciled with the general purport of the Pauline doctrine. The second Epistle attributed to this Clement, although it is from a different hand, after having said that Christ must be regarded *as a God* (a mode of expression which proves that the Church was now gaining its recruits from heathen nations, who hesitated less than the Jews to apply such a name to a created being), teaches in chap. ix. that the Christ, at first spirit, "became flesh," an idea bearing great resemblance to that of an angel who has become man. The Epistles of Ignatius are too uncertain in origin, and the text has been too much altered, to allow of their being taken here into consideration. In the *Shepherd of Hermas*, a curious apocalypse

---

* Such is the name given to some ancient Christian books attributed to such men as Clement of Rome, Barnabas, Ignatius, Polycarp, and Hermas, who, according to tradition, were the immediate followers of the Apostles ; a supposition exceedingly doubtful according to some, and which others think decidedly untrue. All that we can say with certainty is, that they are interesting witnesses to the oscillations of Christian thought from the close of the first century to the end of the second.

which was written at Rome within the first half of the second century, and for a long time held canonical authority, appears a singular Christology. The Son, anterior to the creation, was not Christ, but the Holy Spirit conceived of as a personal being, a kind of archangel. Jesus of Nazareth was his servant, and owed it to his more than perfect obedience that he became associated with this being in dignity and prerogatives.* We can discern in this theory of a writer of decidedly Jew-Christian tendency a marked effort to reconcile the old primitive doctrine with the new opinions. But the idea with him is still that of the man become a Son of God, passed into the state of a "celestial being." In the *Clementine Homilies*, a very remarkable religious romance of the middle of the second century, the Christological doctrine is still more singular, though the author, another Jew-Christian, believed that he was expressing the views of the majority of his time,—as indeed is evident from his urging submission to the bishops. In this book Jesus is no other than the primitive man, who successively appeared as prophet of the truth in Adam, Enoch, Noah, Abraham, Isaac, Jacob, Moses, and finally in Christ. In other words, what is divine in Jesus is the spirit of truth, which employs in addressing men successive instruments; and the writer speaks in strong terms of reprobation of those who, under the plea that Jesus is the Son of God, would apply to him the Divine name.†

* *Simil.* v. 2, ix. 12. † *Hom.* xvi. 5 and seq.

But while, in the Christology of these ancient writers, the chief stress was still laid upon the reality of the human nature and human life of Jesus, in another part of the Christian world opinions respecting his person had taken a flight so idealistic, that his human nature was reduced to nothing more than an unreal phantom. The numerous *Gnostic* systems (systems pretending to a science of religion superior to the common faith), in their dualistic contempt for matter, which they regarded as in itself evil and sinful, generally agreed in saying that Christ was an *æon*,* the redeemer of spiritual men, and that he had but little or no connection at all with corporeal nature. This was the tendency called *Docetism*, which strove in the best way it could to reconcile itself with the evangelical history. Some divided the person of Jesus by separating it from the invisible Christ, who remained a stranger to the temptations, sufferings and death of the man who bore his name; others denied that there had been anything more than outward appearance in all that was related of the human life of Jesus. Valentinus, one of the Gnostic leaders, maintained that the Christ was not born *of* (ἐκ) Mary, but *through* (διά) her

---

* One of the essential features of Gnosticism was also that it filled up the void between God and the material world by a certain number of *æons*, or personifications of the divine ideas, the totality of which constituted the *pleroma*, or plenitude of perfection. Gnosticism formed in the second century the transition between Christianity and Polytheism, just as Jewish-Christianity insensibly turned back towards Judaism. The majority of the Church fluctuated between these two extremes, but not without being influenced by them in more than one respect.

who passed for his mother; his birth, therefore, was not real. Marcion carried Docetism to an extreme, teaching that the Christ had descended suddenly from heaven, having had no connection whatever with the material world. This Docetism, which, like other Christian conceptions of the same age, arose from the desire to glorify the person of Jesus, led to results contrary to its original intention. Would not the consequence certainly follow, that the whole evangelical history, and with it even the religious and moral grandeur of him whom it was desired to glorify, was after all nothing more than a series of false appearances?

This was one of the chief objections which at length brought Gnosticism into disfavour with the Christian majority. But in this very majority there were Christians by no means wanting in the desire to give to their beliefs some speculative, philosophical form, in accordance with the need they felt to exalt, as much as possible, the person of Jesus. The Gnosticism of the second century was only the exaggeration of a tendency shared by almost all religious minds. The claims the Christians put forth grew larger. The new religion made rapid progress, as may be inferred from the often cited letter of Pliny to Trajan. The idea that Jesus had revealed the eternal and universal religion took visible shape in the daily spread of Christianity. The Platonists began to furnish brilliant recruits to the churches of Asia and Greece, and introduced among them their love of system and their idealism. To state the facts in a few words, Hellenism insensibly supplanted Judaism as the form of Christian thought, and to this is mainly owing the orthodox dogma of the deity of Jesus Christ. The same habit of mind which had permitted the fertile genius of Greece to deify the ideal of valour or physical beauty, showed itself once more in its readiness to deify the religious and moral ideal which had been realized in the person of Christ. Hence the rapidity with which a philosophical doctrine of much earlier origin than Christianity, and at first foreign to the Church, was brought into it, and adapted itself so completely to the prevailing Christology as to become identical therewith, and to pass for the belief which had been professed by the disciples of Jesus from the beginning. We have now before us the celebrated doctrine of the Word. We will briefly sketch the history of its formation.

We know that in Platonism the *ideas* of things are their concrete active principles, and any thing whatever exists only in proportion as it is in conformity with its idea. But there is an "idea of existences," their common substance, the principle of being and of truth, God, or the absolute ($\dot{a}\nu\upsilon\pi\acute{o}\theta\epsilon\tau o\nu$). It is this supreme idea which *fashions* the world by moulding the eternal matter according to the particular ideas in which it takes definite form. Everything in the real world that is living and good, everything that develops itself and makes progress, is the work of these divine ideas, of which matter, in itself inert and resistant to their rational force, constitutes the limitation. The Logos, the reason which is in things, like that which is in man, represents therefore the sum of the divine acts by which things are formed; and there is an *idea* or soul of the world, which serves as a mediating agent between God, the absolutely perfect, and imperfect reality.

This theory, which aimed to reconcile the contradiction involved in the co-existence of the imperfect and the perfect, must have been particularly acceptable to the Jews who desired to interpret philosophically the teaching of their own religious traditions. In proportion as the progress of Monotheism had elevated and purified their conception of God, they had felt the difficulty of reconciling with the divine perfection the anthropomorphisms and anthropopathies of the Old Testament. This book had already to a certain degree shown the way by sometimes representing an *angel of the Eternal* as interposing in the place of Jehovah, but speaking and acting in his name.* Some other Jewish books rather assign to *Wisdom* this office of mediator between God and the world, while that which was at first a simple poetic personification gradually assumed the character of a distinct person. We find also an expression employed by the two great divisions of Judaism which gravitated respectively around Jerusalem and Alexandria—in Chaldee the *Memra* or Word of God, in Greek the *Logos*—to designate

* Gen. xxx. 11, 13 ; Exod. iii. 2—7, xiii. 21; comp. xiv. 19, &c.

the being who organized and who governs the world, inferior only to God, who in this theory, as M. Michel Nicolas ingeniously puts it, "reigns and does not govern." The popular Judaism was satisfied to explain the constant relation between God and the world by means of the Holy Spirit, and occasionally angels; and we shall see that later, when the theory of the Logos was generally accepted, there was a difficulty in distinguishing the action of the Word in the world from that of the Holy Spirit. The question may also be asked whether the impulse which determined Judaism towards this particular doctrine was of Mazdean or of Hellenic origin. It might easily have proceeded from either of these currents, both of which so powerfully influenced the theological development of Judaism. But, at the exact period in history which we have reached, it cannot now be maintained that any considerable effect was produced by the purely Jewish theology on the Christian, which, on the contrary, came more and more under the influence of Greek ideas. It is then in the Platonizing, that is the Alexandrian branch of Judaism that we must seek for the antecedents of the Christian doctrine of the Word.

The idea or soul of the Platonic world, taken in its concrete unity, was the divine reason ($\theta\epsilon\hat{\iota}os$ $\lambda\acute{o}\gamma os$), and this reason proceeded directly from God. The Alexandrian theology, of which the celebrated Philo was the chief representative, took this notion of the divine Logos for the centre of its religious conceptions, and, using the word Logos in its twofold acceptation, as signifying sometimes *reason* and sometimes *word*, it distinguished in God the Logos, or *internal* Word (ἐνδιάθετος), the idea of the world conceived by Him from all eternity, and the Logos, or *uttered* Word, *sent forth* (προφορικός). In this the internal Word had become objective, exterior to God from the moment when He sent it forth from himself by an ineffable generation (γέννησις), in order to proceed by its means not to create, but to give form and development to the world. For Philo also, with the Platonists, considers matter to be eternal, formless, and by itself incapable of development and life. The Word, therefore, as now exterior to God, but co-essential with the author of its distinct being, is called ὁ δεύτερος θεός, the second God; ὁ θεὸς ἐν καταχρήσει, God not in the proper sense; θεός without the article, that is to say a being of divine essence, God in the collective sense, to distinguish him from the supreme God, from Him who alone is God in the full force of the term, ὁ ἀληθείᾳ Θεός. From the moment when the Word is sent forth from the bosom of the Father, it is also called the eldest or first-born Son of God (υἱὸς πρεσβύτατος, πρωτόγονος τοῦ Θεοῦ). Its distinct existence, therefore, is coincident in point of time with the moment preceding the first formation of the world, that is, with the moment when, according to Genesis, "God SAID."

Thus nearly about the same time when Jesus was

proclaiming the *fatherhood* of God as expressive of his real relation to mankind, Philo, his contemporary, was teaching the metaphysical *fatherhood* of God, to explain the connection between the Creator and the creation. But the resemblance was only superficial. In place of the living God, the Inspirer of humanity, the Father in direct and constant communication with the world and man, Philo substituted a God withdrawn into the depths of abstraction, delegating the government of the world to a vicegerent. He it is who reveals himself to men; who is the unique source of life, truth, and happiness, and who specially made use of the people of Israel to communicate these to the world; who appeared to the patriarchs and to Moses; who spoke by the prophets; who is, in a word, the organ of the divine activity throughout the numberless vicissitudes of the world and of history.

Considering these facts, when we remember what we have seen of the progress of Christian belief as to the person of Jesus, we can easily understand that the day was sure to arrive when this personality, in its ascent towards perfect deity, would come into contact with the Alexandrian theory of the Logos, and would for a time be identified with the " God of the second order" assumed by Philo. The latest evolutions of the Pauline theology will have already prepared us for this result. The course of ideas and events in the first half of the second century ended by giving to the doctrine of the Word an established position within the Christian Church, and we may witness for ourselves the grand solemnity of its naturalization in the nearly contemporary but independent works of two Christian writers of this epoch, Justin Martyr, and the author of the fourth Gospel.

Justin, called the Martyr, a native of Palestine, but a Greek by education, an evangelist under the mantle of a philosopher, wrote two *Apologies* for the Christian faith, which he had adopted after much fruitless trial of other systems, and a *Dialogue* with the Jew Trypho, against whom he maintained the Messianic and divine character of Jesus. As a man of but average intelligence, more sincere than enlightened, and disliking all extremes, he may be taken to represent the main body of the Christians of his time, and his martyrdom at Rome under Marcus Aurelius, towards the year 166, gave additional value to his writings. The influence of the religious philosophy of Alexandria upon his theology is evident. His God is the abstract, inexplicable being, and it is the Logos, or the Word, which, proceeding from the bosom of God (where it existed before all time, and was thrown forth from Him at a given moment by an effort of his power and will), must fill up the abyss existing in thought between the infinite and the finite, the incomprehensible absolute and the world perceptible to sense. God did not grow less by sending the Word forth from himself, any more than a flame grows less by lighting another flame. God made use of his Word to organize formless matter,*

* *Apol.* i. 24 and 29.

and above all to reveal Himself to men. It is this Word, in fact, which, diffused among the sages of antiquity, but more concentrated in the prophets of Israel, has communicated the truth to the world.

However, the ideas of Justin are wanting in precision. There are passages in his writings in which the Word, which logically should be unique in its kind, as having been begotten directly from the very essence of God, is compared to the angels,* or is no more than the firstborn of the beings formed by the divine will, or the first of the forces (δυνάμεις) which emanated from the absolute power.† Justin, it is true, is careful to mark strongly the distinction between the Word and the true God, ὁ ὄντως Θεός,‡ and to establish clearly its subordination. The Son is only the "servant of the Father;" he is *God*, but only by the will of the Father; the only unity that exists between them is that of agreement of will (γνώμη),§ the will of the Son always submitting to that of the Father; he only comes after the Father in dignity.‖ Like Philo, Justin distinguishes θεός, god, without the article, from ὁ θεός, God, with the article. What is new in him is, that he decidedly identifies this Son with the person of Jesus. The Word, which inspired the great philosophers and the prophets, appeared at last under the form and conditions of a human life, to

---

* *Apol.* i. 6.   † *Apol.* i. 23, 32, 63 ; *Tryph.* 61, 62.
‡ *Apol.* i. 13.   § *Tryph.* 56, 62, 129.
‖ *Apol.* i. 12, 13, 32, 60 ; *Apol.* ii. 13.

teach men definitively the truth and the moral law. There are then, in fact, with Justin two Gods, the one superior, the other inferior; and it is characteristic of him that he so little concerned himself to inquire how far this ditheism could be reconciled with the monotheism common to both the Christian and Jewish faiths. The complete subordination in which he places the Son in presence of the Father, appears to him to suffice for the preservation of the Divine unity. This proves how greatly the Hellenistic view now prevailed over the Jewish in the Christian Church.*

The theology of Justin was wanting in another respect. Without entering into the lengthened discussions that have arisen respecting the Gospels used by him, we may lay it down as an established fact that Justin was not acquainted with our fourth Gospel, but had, amongst other documents, a Gospel, now lost, which possessed some features that have been reproduced also in this one. Had Justin known this, he would evidently have made the most frequent use of it, and his manner of relating the earthly history of the Word would have been very sensibly influenced by it. Now Justin, when speaking of the life of Jesus, always adheres closely to the limits and point of view of the first Gospels. Yet there was something incongruous, and even con-

---

* If we compare the long discussions of Peter and Simon Magus in the *Clementine Homilies* upon the unity of God, and the impropriety of giving the name of God to any one but the Father, we shall have an idea of the change which had come over Christian opinion with respect to this subject.

tradictory, between the narratives of these Gospels and the theory of the Word. The Logos, being pre-existent and of divine essence, could not consistently be born, or grow up, or suffer, or be tempted, or receive divine attributes as a reward, like the Christ of primitive tradition. If any one desired to make the doctrine of the Word really apply to the person of Jesus, he must reconstruct the evangelical history, understanding it henceforth in this speculative view which accorded so well with the desire of the Christians to give increasing honour to their Master and Saviour. The necessity of this historical revision was more clearly seen by one of Justin's contemporaries, a Philonist like himself, but more mystical, more profound, and bolder, who, about the time when the philosopher was publishing his *Apologies* at Rome, brought out a new Gospel in Asia Minor; allowing it to be understood that the history contained in his pages was derived from the testimony of the most intimate, the most faithful disciple of Jesus,—that of John the beloved, who had laid his head on the Master's bosom, and whose statements, consequently, must be of more value than those of the humble chroniclers who until then had been the sole collectors of the popular traditions respecting the person and work of Christ.

The great object which the last Evangelist had in his writings was to apply the idea of the Word to the Gospel history. For if, as has often been said, he had only meant to strike a blow at the Gnostic doctrines, it would be very strange that he should have sanctioned in several instances, rather than attacked, certain fundamental Gnostic tenets. The mode of procedure adopted by this writer offers no grounds of surprise to any person who is acquainted with antiquity and its literary habits; and the new Gospel coincided so entirely with the tendencies and prepossessions of Christendom, that, in spite of some opposition, which, however, called forth little response, it soon became widely known, and was everywhere regarded as equally primitive with, and not less historical than, the other Gospels. It was chiefly by its means that the doctrine of the Word, and of its identity with the person of Jesus, became Christian dogma.

One of the most unassailable results of the biblical criticism of our time is the demonstration it has furnished of the systematically formed plan of the anonymous historian, and of his unvarying purpose, carried out with rare ability, to eliminate from the evangelical history whatever tended to compromise the doctrine of the Word, while introducing on the other hand many new elements designed to confirm it. Moreover, he himself makes no secret of his design, of which indeed he gives clear notice to the reader in a prologue completely impregnated with Philonist expressions and ideas. The Logos-God ($\theta\epsilon\acute{o}s$) is, at the beginning of things, present as a distinct being with God ($\pi\rho\grave{o}s$ $\tau\grave{o}\nu$ $\Theta\epsilon\acute{o}\nu$). All things became what they are ($\dot{\epsilon}\gamma\acute{\epsilon}\nu\epsilon\tau o$) by him, not *were created* ($\dot{\epsilon}\kappa\tau\acute{\iota}\sigma\theta\eta$), and nothing that has so become is without his action (i. 1—3). In him is life, and the life is the light of men; but the darkness, the material, negative element, in itself rebellious against the divine action, repels the light, and from thence arises the permanent conflict between the luminous divine action and the dark Satanic reaction, a conflict of which the incarnation of the Word marks the decisive crisis. In effect, the Word or the only Son (μονογενής), he who alone **is** directly begotten from God, who alone is in a position **to** reveal to man the divine mysteries, has made a human body his **tent,** his temporary dwelling-place (ἐσκήνωσεν ἐν ἡμῖν), and has appeared under this covering living amongst men. **The** Platonic dualism which penetrates this entire conception of things is applied to the human race also. **In** presence of the incarnate Word, men are divided into "children of light" and "children of darkness." The Word delivers the children of light **out** of the power of the devil, *the prince of this world.** It is for this very purpose that he has become incarnate, that, **by** virtue of the elective affinity which draws like **to** like, **the** children of darkness should go to perdition, whilst the children of light will spontaneously **obey the** attractive power of the Word which communicates **to them** his divine spirit.

The whole **of this** theology is of a kind quite foreign to **the** primitive evangelical history. Hence also it is that, **in** this Gospel alone, Jesus speaks of himself as of a

---

* John xii. 31, xiv. 30, xvii. 15.

being who has a clear consciousness of having existed prior to his coming upon earth, and who was soon to re-enter upon the possession of the incomparable glory which he already had before the world was.* The Word gives proof during his visible manifestation on earth, as indeed it is fitting that he should, that he possesses omniscience,† and an absolute power over nature. There is no question here of development in him. From the first moment he knows that he is the only Son, perfect in all respects, superior to every trial. A temptation like that in the wilderness, an outward transfiguration like that of Tabor, a mental agony like that of Gethsemane, are entirely outside the logical framework of the fourth Gospel, and are indirectly denied in certain passages.‡ The very title of Son of Man has lost its human significance; it has become synonymous with Son of God.§ The Word-Jesus can therefore present himself before the world as the author and the necessary centre of all religious and moral life.‖ To refuse allegiance to him is to decide voluntarily, by that very act, for error and evil. He could not, like the Jesus of the Synoptics, admit that any one might speak against him without speaking against the Holy Spirit. He suffers one of the disciples to address him with an exclamation of

---

* John viii. 58, xvii. 5.   † Ibid. i. 47, 48, iv. 16—18, &c.
‡ Ibid. i. 14, 35, xii. 27.
§ Ibid. xi. 4; comp. iii. 13, vi. 38, 62, xiii. 31.
‖ Ibid. v. 21, 26, vi. 33, seq., xi. 25, seq. &c.

mingled repentance and awe as his *Lord* and his *God*.*
In a word, such is his glory, that he considers it fitting
to observe to his disciples that his Father is greater
than he,† as if they could have doubted the fact.

This passsage, by the way, is not an isolated one in
this Gospel, which subordinates the Son to the Father
quite as decidedly as Justin does. The Father alone is
the true God, God in the absolute sense (ὁ μόνος ἀληθινὸς
Θεός).‡ If the Son says that he is *one* (ἕν) with the Father,
this can only be understood of moral union, since it is
to extend also to his disciples (xvii. 22). The Son can
do nothing of himself; he is submissive and obedient,
and repudiates all intention of making himself equal
with God. Thus he can only be called *god* in a restricted
sense, higher no doubt, but in reality analogous to that
in which the name was applied to the judges of Israel.§
The passages which attest this inferiority are very
numerous; and, besides, the imperfection which permits
of its holding relations with the world and with men,
incompatible with the absolute perfection of the Father,
belongs to the very conception of the Word. Thus the
flesh of the Word can endure all the wants, sensations,
and sufferings, of every human body. Its ψυχή, its fleshly
soul (according to the Platonic psychology which distinguished this from the rational soul) can be troubled, but
not its spirit, its person properly so called; and it is

* John xx. 28. † Ibid. xiv. 28.
‡ John xvii. 3. § Ibid. v. 17—19, x. 33—38.

very remarkable that the single exception which can be pointed out, a passage in which it is said that Jesus "was troubled in his spirit,"* is only an apparent one. Anger, in fact, in this Gospel, is among the dispositions proper to the Divine Mind.†

With the fourth Gospel and Justin Martyr, the Christian faith accomplished an evolution, which consisted in substituting for the idea of a man become divine that of a divine being becoming man. The application of the theory of the Word to the person of Jesus was made therefore without a concerted purpose, and it resulted from the general movement of opinion. The unknown author of the *Epistle of Diognetus* (ch. vii.), who must have been almost the contemporary of both, also gives to the Christ the title of Word. What a strange destiny is that of Jesus! The world contends about the question as to who shall bestow upon him the most august crown. Judaism did not conceive that there could exist upon earth a being superior to the Messiah of its expectations, and Jews confer upon him this to them incomparable title; whilst Hellenism, as the end of its philosophical

---

* John xi. 33, ἐνεβριμήσατο τῷ πνεύματι. Thus the words of v. 35, *Jesus wept*, could not relate to the grief which Jesus felt at the tomb of his friend Lazarus. Taken in connection with the whole plan of the work, this incident signifies that Jesus wept over the unbelief and opposition of which his word was the object; it was the result of the ἐμβρίμησις of which he spoke twice, v. 33 and 38, and not of the death of Lazarus, whom he was going immediately to raise.

† John iii. 36.

speculations, discovers a divine being superior to everything in the whole world, and it can do no other than identify this being with the humble Son of Man. Nothing appears extravagant to Christendom in its enthusiasm for the person of Jesus as identified with the new ideal which he revealed. But Christian opinion is yet far from having reached its resting-place on the path which it has appeared its duty to take. It is committed to complete ditheism, in which, though it may long remain, it cannot continue always. The great question is, how will it emerge from this? Will it have the courage to retrace its steps, or, on the other hand, will it advance yet further? The following chapters will give the reply.

CHAPTER IV.

DITHEISM AND THE UNITARIAN PROTEST.

In the latter half of the second century, and through the whole of the third, the doctrine of the Word incarnate became increasingly popular, until at the close of this period it attained to the position of an official doctrine, an ecclesiastical dogma. The Church, as it constantly grew in numbers and in power, endeavoured so to organize itself as to acquire an outward form which should respond to its eager craving for unity, and to secure this by unity in the doctrine everywhere professed. Though it asserted its own independence of the Empire, the imperial unity nevertheless awed and fascinated it, and it would seem to have foreseen the day when the Empire and the Church would be one. The oligarchical constitution of the episcopate, henceforth invested with the rights which the whole body of Christians formerly possessed, and the strict determination of the doctrine which should alone be held divine and legitimate, were the fruits of this double tendency. Hence arose the earliest Catholicism, which was not yet Roman, and might rather be considered Greek in this respect, that the centre of gravity, the active life, the great writers of the Church, were to be found in the East rather than in the West; but which was already imperial in tendency, and only awaited the hour when it would be so in fact.

And thus did an early and a very important modification of Christianity take place. From the conception in the mind of its Founder of a religion of the conscience and the heart, originally assuming, as the only condition of communion with God, feelings and spiritual dispositions which readily associate with very different beliefs, Christianity became an *orthodoxy*, a religion in which the question of *belief* took the precedence of every other. Henceforth the holding of the truth became more essential than the practice of holiness; since from the orthodox point of view sin is pardonable, error is not. The Church consequently believed itself called above all things to present the true doctrine to the faithful, the "doctrine of salvation," apart from which could be nothing but perdition. It was for the bishops (who were still all on an equality, though considerable deference was paid to the more important sees) henceforth to decide what was necessary to be believed, or not believed, *on pain of anathema*. The opposition of the Montanists (a body of austere *illuminati* who held in greater respect the inspired teaching of individuals under religious ecstacy, than the mere numbers of the bishops) gradually became more feeble. From a period dating before the middle of the third century they cease to claim historical consideration.

It is clear that this love of dogmatic truth the possession of which was considered indispensable to salvation, harmonized wonderfully with the doctrine of the Word, which became pre-eminently the episcopal, the *ecclesiastical* doctrine. The Church was henceforth the grand depository of eternal truth. Its bishops, bearing the sole charge of dispensing it, were in the eyes of the mass of Christians the rightful conservators of the apostolic tradition. This tradition, again, was reputed entirely to consist of revelations made to his apostles by the great Revealer, the Logos, that divine Word which alone possessed such intimate knowledge of God as to be able to unveil to men with authority the mysteries of the celestial world.* Thus everything seemed well organized to this end, that the truth, truth only, the whole truth, should come from heaven to earth through the channel of the Church, that is to say of the bishops. It may be permitted to us to doubt whether the theory of the Word would so readily have become the cherished doctrine of Christendom, if the Church had continued faithful to the Christianity of Jesus, or even if it had been at this time what it afterwards became, a thoroughly sacerdotal institution. In the former case the human sanctity of Jesus, in the latter his dignity as Priest or Redeemer, would have rather attracted the interest of the faithful, and the investigations of the learned. It followed from the turn things actually took, that the nature and the absolute authority of Jesus as revealer absorbed Christian thought, and determined the course of opinion about his person.†

The incomplete and in many respects still very vague form of the theory of the Word, as Justin Martyr and the fourth Evangelist had presented it, necessarily, by the simple reason of the ever-growing favour attach-

---

* Comp. John vi. 46.

† If it is asked what was the still deeper cause which thus plunged the Church into orthodoxy, I think it must be sought in its permanent conflict with the heathenism in face of which, from the beginning, it upheld rational truth in opposition to world-old superstition. Hence its preponderating intellectual tendency. We may observe the same thing in the attitude of an orthodoxy which the Protestant Church so early assumed in its struggle with the religion of the middle ages.

ing to its essential principle, called for more ample explanations and developments. This was not the work of a day. In the latter half of the second century such writers as Tatian, an enthusiastic follower of Justin's, Athenagoras, who undertook the defence of Christianity before Marcus Aurelius, and Theophilus of Antioch (170—180), preached this doctrine with variations of thought and expression which prove how far it was from being settled. We may notice, however, in particular, four writers who, at the end of the second century and the commencement of the third, gave the most authoritative direction to Christian thought; Irenæus, bishop of Lyons, Tertullian, the fiery presbyter of Carthage, Clement of Alexandria, and Origen.

Irenæus was strongly opposed to Gnosticism, supremely devoted to ecclesiastical unity, and extremely timid with regard to speculation on religious subjects. He contributed much by his writings and his influence to set the seal of orthodoxy on this famous doctrine, but he neither threw much light upon it, nor perfected it. The preceding writers regarded the Word as having emanated at a certain point of duration from the Father. Irenæus finds this assertion too bold, and the expression *emanate* too Gnostic. He preferred to be silent, rather than attempt to define the moment when the Word became external, or a person, having been previously internal, and not yet given forth.* On the other hand,

* *Adv. Hær.* ii. 28.

he so attenuated the distinction of person between the Father and the Son, that at times it becomes entirely imperceptible. To say that the Son is "the visible" form of the Father, and the Father "the invisible" of the Son,* is almost to deny the personality of both, reducing them to two modes or aspects of the same God. A representation corresponding with this may be deduced from the comparison, which he frequently made, of the Son and the Holy Spirit to the "two hands of God."† This would involve the conception, not of two personal beings, but of organs, in themselves unconscious. The theology of Irenæus thus ran the risk of falling upon the rock of the Sabellian Unitarianism of which we shall presently speak—the more so because, in his views of redemption, he urgently insisted upon the idea that human nature, being corrupt by means of and since Adam, must be saved by being presented to God pure and holy in the person of its second head, the Christ. The Son of God, he said, became man in order that man might become a Son of God;‡ so that virtually there is a unity of nature between man and the Word. Human nature, however, even when realizing all the perfection of which it is capable, has sufferings to bear which are irreconcilable with the Divine nature. Irenæus felt this so strongly (iii. 19, 3), that he separated the man Jesus from the Word incar-

* Adv. Hær. iv. 6, 6. † Ibid. iv. Pref. iv. 20, 1 et alius.
‡ Ibid. iii. 10, 2, 19, 1 et alias.

nate in him, going so far as to say that the Word *rested* (ἡσυχάζοντος τοῦ Λόγου), while Jesus was tempted, was crucified, and died. What then becomes, with Irenæus, of the historical person of Jesus? On how dangerous an incline his orthodoxy is on the point of being carried away! But we must forbear to apply the measure of a too rigid interpretation to an author who in a manner affects the indefinite and vague.

Tertullian, writing very soon afterwards, displays a character of mind totally different. For him there was nothing obscure or difficult, nothing that did not adjust itself wonderfully well in the theory of the Word incarnate. So sure was he of what he asserted, that it would seem as if he had been permitted to contemplate the manner of procedure pursued by the Deity with regard to Himself and the world. With his materialistic turn of mind, he felt no embarrassment at the idea that, at a certain moment, God became a Father by a kind of "casting forth" from his eternal substance.* *Fuit tempus cum et delictum et filius non fuit, quod judicem et qui patrem Dominum faceret,* "Time was when there was neither sin nor son to make the Lord a judge or a father," said he bluntly to Hermogenes (ch. iii.), who ounded his doctrine of the eternity of the world on that of the immutability of God. This is precisely the formula which the Arianism of a later period adopted.

* For the ideas of Tertullian as a whole, see the article entitled *Tertullien et la Montanisme* in the *Revue des Deux Mondes* for Nov. 1, 1864.

On the other hand, with Tertullian, the doctrine of the Word freed itself from the dualism with which it was infected under its earlier form. It was not from pre-existing matter that the creatures were formed by the Divine action. Tertullian knew also the precise period at which the generation of the Word took place, namely, just at the moment when God pronounced the *Fiat Lux* of Genesis.* By appearing to the patriarchs and inspiring the prophets, the Son *accustomed himself* to live with men,† and as he was an inferior God, the Old Testament could easily attribute to him those anthropomorphisms in which a too cautious reason would find it difficult to recognize the Father, the Being who may be described as God philosophically conceived, in consideration of his absolute perfection.‡ And so Tertullian uses with reference to the Word, without any distinction, the expressions *made, created, begotten*, which do not present to his eyes any essential difference in signification.§ The Son is, according to him, an extension, a radiation, from the Father, a *derivatio totius*;‖ and it was this inferior God who, *delapsus in virginem quamdam*, took the flesh of man. Such is with him the *corporatio Dei;* and he often expresses

---

* *Adv. Prax.* 7.
† Ibid. 16. This rather curious idea is found previously in Irenæus, *Adv. Hær.* iv. 12, 4.
‡ *Ut ita dixerim, philosophorum Deus.* Adv. Mark ii. 27.
§ *Filios facimus, licet generemus,* he says to Hermogenes, 32.
‖ *Adv. Prax.* 9.

himself as if there had been in Jesus only the Word and a human body, although in other places, on the contrary, he speaks as if Jesus had also had a human soul. It should be noted here that, by his theory of the Divine essence, according to which the Holy Spirit, the second and last emanation from God, is not distinct from the Father and the Son until after the Pentecost, he unconsciously but seriously compromises or alters the evangelical tradition. It might be said, according to this view, that the Word had conceived itself in the womb of Mary. All these peculiar opinions as to the strongly-marked inferiority of the Son, his birth in time, the quite recent emission of the Holy Spirit, &c., show that Tertullian was an irreclaimable heretic according to the standard of later orthodoxy; but not the less did he open the way to this orthodoxy by insisting, much more than yet had been done, upon the identity of substance between the Father and the Son. The latter, he said, is *light issued from light, lumen de lumine;* and this comparison, which owed its dogmatic value to the ignorance of the ancients on the indefinite transmission of light, received the ultimate sanction of the Church.

In another respect Tertullian was among the ancestors of the orthodoxy of the Councils. He was the first to teach in complete form a Divine *Trinity*. The Christians, from the commencement of the second century, made use of a characteristic *trilogy*, in which the Father was Creator, the Son founder of the kingdom of God, and the Holy Spirit the agent of God for the salvation of men.* But nothing fixed, nothing dogmatically determined, was as yet implied by these three terms, which were susceptible of so many definitions. Theophilus of Antioch, an Eastern writer at the end of the second century, introduced into ecclesiastical terminology the expression *triad* (τριάς), which was afterwards used as the Greek equivalent of the Latin word *trinitas*, without, however, expressing its full force. It was Tertullian who invented the word *trinity* to describe the God of his creed, *triple* as to the persons composing it, but *one* in substance, as well as by the absolute superiority of the first term in the series, that is, of the Father. We know the pre-eminent place that the Trinity, conceived, it is true, quite differently, has since occupied in the Christian belief. But at the time of which we are speaking, we must confine ourselves to noticing the origination of the word, the germ of the idea. Christendom as yet thought very little about it. The third term, the Holy Spirit, was not the subject of any controversy. Some looked upon it as a person, others as the action of God upon the soul. The Greek word *pneuma*, with its sense of *breath* and its neuter gender, countenanced the latter acceptation, while the pagan propensity to multiply divine personages rather favoured

---

* This trilogy first appears as the formula of baptism at the end of the Gospel of Matthew, xxviii. 19. Its original signification is therefore indicated by the contents of the book which first gives it.

the former. But we must wait till the close of the fourth century to find the question of the personality of the Holy Spirit, and its relation to the Father and the Son, at last plainly presented and decided upon by the Church.

It was neither, however, in Africa nor in the East that the Trinitarian doctrine was to attain its completion. Alexandria, the home of Philonism and Neo-Platonism, was naturally destined to serve as a central factory for the elaboration of the dogma of the deity of Jesus Christ. In that city, throughout the third century, flourished a school of transcendental theology, which though it came afterwards to be regarded with considerable suspicion by the jealous conservators of ecclesiastical doctrine, was not the less on that account the real cradle of orthodoxy. It was the Platonic tendency that influenced the religious speculations of Clement, Origen, and Dionysius: the theory of the Word, which originated in their city, constituted the permanent framework of their theology.*

Clement, who flourished at the close of the first century and the beginning of the second, yielded to no

---

* This school developed side by side with the Neo-Platonic school of Plotinus, Porphyry, and Jamblicus (200—300), which also had its triad, the *One*, the *Thought*, and the *Soul*. But if it is certain beforehand that the two sister schools could not have existed together without influencing each other, it may be seen by all that has preceded that we should be wrong in regarding the Christian Trinity as borrowed, purely and simply, from the Neo-Platonism of the third century.

Platonist in his disposition to exalt the idea of God to such a point that it ended in becoming a pure and empty abstraction. It was for this reason that he held firmly by the doctrine of the Word, which offered to him, if an imperfect God, yet one who could be spoken about and comprehended. On the other hand, his *Word* stood so high, that he could scarcely reconcile its august character with the facts of the evangelical history. Great obscurity rests upon his views relative to the historical person of the Christ. Occasionally he appears to fall into complete Docetism. He maintains, for example, that if Jesus ate and drank, it was in condescension to men, and that in reality his body was sustained by a supernatural force.[*] In one place he broaches the opinion that the Saviour suffered no pain during the hours of his passion. When it is remembered that Clement of Alexandria is counted in the number of the canonized saints of the Church, it must be confessed that orthodoxy has singularly changed its character since the third century.

His influence was nevertheless very powerful in the propagation of the doctrine of the Word. But still greater was that of his illustrious disciple, Origen, the grandest name in the Church of the third century. Origen was the first to lay down a vast system of theology, one singularly bold and very original, and supported by an erudition at that time rare. But so strong

---

[*] *Strom.* vi. 9.

was the impulse which controlled the course of Christian thought, that although the number of his devoted disciples was very great, nothing of his system survived him but such portions as fell in with the current of the orthodox ecclesiastical tendency.

He contributed to the formation of the future orthodoxy by teaching, with a decisive firmness before unknown, that the Word, or the Son, is eternal. It is true that, as his system insisted much upon the immutability of God, created things and souls were also in his view eternal; so that this eternity attributed to the Word did not specifically separate him from other creatures. With Origen, the idea of God was not so much resolved, as it was with Clement, into a pure abstraction. He was opposed, therefore, to the idea that the Father and the Son were of the same substance,* since the one was absolutely perfect, while the other possessed only an acquired and contingent perfection, and owed his existence simply to an act of the Father's will.† He declares very plainly the inferiority of the Son to the Father, and reduces his unity with God to oneness in a moral sense.‡

In this system Jesus was man, certainly eternal, but only as we are, and like us in his nature. The great difference was, that during the period of his celestial

---

* In John xx. 16, κατ' οὐσίαν καὶ καθ' ὑποκείμενόν ἐστιν ὁ υἱὸς ἕτερος τοῦ πατρός. In *Joh.* § 2.

† *De Princip.* i. 2, 6.   ‡ *Contra Cels.* viii. 12.

existence, and before he appeared upon earth, his will, which was always good, had so united him to the divine Word, that he was entirely penetrated by it, and became one with it.* The singularly weak point in the system was, that, as the pre-existing souls became human, and so were confined in a body, only in consequence of moral declension, it was impossible to comprehend how the perfectly holy soul of Jesus could have become incarnate. Origen tried in vain to get over this difficulty by alleging that the body of Jesus was in reality much more perfect, more celestial, than ours. This ethereal perfection could only be perceived at brief moments by some chosen spirits, as, for example, on the occasion of the transfiguration; but then, it might be replied, was it a true human body, and does not this lead directly to Docetism?

Origen was essentially a Unitarian. Stated summarily his views amount to this, that Jesus is one of ourselves united to the Deity in the closest manner by his moral sublimity. But the view in which ordinary Unitarianism regards the earthly life of Jesus he extended to the celestial regions. This somewhat fanciful aspect of his system, and these ideas so contrary to the later orthodoxy, which indeed, in conjunction with his favourite doctrine of a final re-union of all creatures in God, afterwards caused his writings and his memory to be condemned, had but a temporary influence on the for-

---

* *De Princip.* ii. 6, 3; *C. Cels.* iii. 41.

mation of the ecclesiastical dogma. On the other hand, the grand position which Origen assigned to the Word, as revealer of the truth amongst the Hebrews and the great philosophers of antiquity, and the eternity which he attributed to it, became more definitely than ever integral parts of the ecclesiastical doctrine then forming.

Alike, therefore, in the East and in the West, the doctrine of the Word, with its application to the person of Jesus, was accepted, although with great diversities in detail, by learned men of influence. Yet it would be erroneous to suppose that it met with no opposition from a considerable number of Christians who were alarmed to see the Church abandoning the principle of strict Monotheism, which it professed in common with Judaism, which Jesus had so forcibly maintained, and for which so many Christians, cruelly persecuted by an irrational polytheism, had shed their blood as martyrs. The doctrine of a god of second rank incarnate in Jesus appeared to them, and not without reason, to be a degenerating into pure ditheism. It was in vain that the advocates of the Word protested against this accusation, pointing to the supremacy of the Father, and either the unity of essence between the Father and the Son, or their moral unity of intention and will; their opponents could readily adduce arguments in justification of the reply that these considerations in no way solved the difficulty. Could not polytheism itself claim on the same terms the honour of being monotheistic? Had it not its supreme God, as well as gods sharing in common the Divine nature, and necessarily obeying their head? Unitarianism, in the second and third centuries, was a very important element in the Christian Church. It had its watchword, the *Monarchy*, and, according to Tertullian,* it could boast of being the belief of the majority of that period. *Monarchiam tenemus,* "we hold to the Monarchy," proudly exclaimed the Western Unitarians, who delighted to mingle Greek words with their religious phraseology. Tertullian ridicules their pronunciation, which was probably affected by the difficulty with which they articulated the aspirate *ch* of the Greek. Bringing Greek against Greek, therefore, he proposed the singular expression, *economy* (οἰκονομία), or *distribution,* of the Divine Being, in order to represent the idea of the Father putting himself forth successively in the Son and the Holy Spirit.† But it does not appear that the *gloriosissima multitudo* was thereby persuaded, which had taken the Divine *monarchy* as its chosen standard.

It must, however, be added, that Unitarianism was

---

* *Adv. Prax.* 10.

† Tertullian's predilection for the Greek evidently prevented him from using the Latin word *dispositio*, which would have served much better as an abstract term. And if he chose to speak Greek, I strongly suspect that Tertullian did not select the word *diathesis* because that word, on account of the aspirate *th*, which should be pronounced somewhat like the English *th*, was not more familiar in Latin speech than the *ch* of the favourite Unitarian term. The word proposed by Tertullian took no permanent hold.

so unfortunate as to have been often presented in antiquated or in gross forms, which could not recommend it either to thinkers or to the many Christians who, without pretending to philosophy, were sensible of the attractions of a broad and elevated doctrine.

Thus the old Jew-Christian Unitarianism, the orthodoxy of primitive days, being closely bound up with Jewish observances, was confined to the descendants of the converted Jews in Palestine, Syria, and the Decapolis. Incapable of expansion, while the universal Church was undergoing a transformation which was preparing it to meet its glorious destinies, these communities, which are so interesting from their origin, quietly fell into contempt through narrowness and superstition. In their turn they became heretical and separate from the rest of Christendom. They remained, that is to say, what they had always been, while everything was changing around them. They were always distinguished as Nazarenes, the name first given by the Jews to the disciples of Jesus. They preferred to call themselves Ebionites, or the *poor;** and several writers, prompted by the vulgar prejudice that every divergence from sound doctrines proceeds from some individual defection, and forgetting that the term had been sometimes used as a generic name for all Christians, had already invented for them a founder, a heresiarch of the name of *Ebion*, who never

---

* From the Hebrew *Ebionim*, in allusion, no doubt, to the poverty extolled in Matt. v. 3. Comp. Eusebius, *Hist. Eccles.* iii. 27.

existed at all but in the imagination of the Catholic Fathers. The only reason for regretting the almost total loss of their special literature is, that they must have possessed some very curious documents relating to the early days of Christianity, while some remarkable works, translations and expositions of the Old Testament, were produced amongst them. Theodotion, Symmachus, and Aquila, the authors of certain versions of the sacred books which were held of some repute, belonged to the Judaizing Church. In their controversies they reaped great advantage from their knowledge of the original texts. They had corrected, for example, to the great offence of Justin Martyr and the Christian doctors who did not understand Hebrew, the inaccurate translation in the Septuagint of the passage in Isaiah vii. 14, and showed with great reason that, in what was believed to be the prediction of the miraculous birth of a virgin's son, the prophet was only speaking of the approaching deliverance of a young woman. There were, however, some Jew-Christians who, with our first canonical Evangelist, admitted without difficulty the miraculous birth of Jesus, but would not hear of his pre-existence. The name of Nazarenes was usually given in preference to those moderate Ebionites who stood somewhat less apart than the others from the rest of Christendom.* But neither had any influence whatever. They were reproached with thinking of the

* Comp. Gieseler, *Kirchengesch.* Vol. i. p. 131.

Christ πτωχὸς καὶ ταπεινῶς, *poorly and meanly*. That was quite enough to say. Their kind of Unitarianism made no more proselytes than did their persistency in regarding the Apostle Paul as a blasphemer and an apostate. Suffering encroachments little by little from the larger Church, or through ephemeral Gnostic tendencies, these Christians of the earliest type disappeared in the seventh century without the fact attracting any attention.

There were other forms of Unitarian doctrine which moved Christendom more profoundly. The same somewhat pagan spirit which urged many Christians to make much of the doctrine of the personal Word, and to identify this with the person of Jesus, led many others to teach that Jesus was purely and simply God in a human form, and that there was no ground for making a distinction of persons between the Father and the Son. If Monotheism was preserved in this view, the same could not be said of either the spirituality or the perfection of the Divine Being, since it must then be admitted that the Father had been tempted, had suffered, and died; and hence the name of *Patripassionism* given to this doctrine. One of the most celebrated of its representatives, Praxeas, who was sent to Rome by the bishops of Asia towards the close of the second century, for the purpose of explaining to the Roman bishop the true character of the Montanist movement, appears to have been very well received in the eternal city, to the great indignation of Tertullian, which he expressed in one of his most virulent writings. But there may be reason to think that the fiery African Montanist misrepresented to some extent the doctrine of Praxeas. There are indications which would justify the supposition that he was not so much a *Patripassionist* as an *Alogist*, that is, an adherent of a school about which very little is known, but that seems to have controverted for some time in Asia Minor the authority of the fourth Gospel and the Philonist theory of the Logos. The probability is, that, like the Hermas of whom we have already spoken, Praxeas maintained the old Christology, according to which the Son was the man Jesus fully inspired, possessed, if we may venture so to speak, by the Spirit of God. But as it bluntly characterized the human nature of Jesus by the expressions *body* and *flesh*, the impassioned adversaries of this doctrine, as well as its less enlightened partisans, might easily believe that it enclosed in the body of the Christ, God the Creator in person, and so subjected him to all the miseries of humanity. We shall understand this view better if we remember how common in the churches of the two first centuries was a state of ecstacy in which the "possession" of the individual by the Divine Spirit appeared to suppress the distinct personal consciousness, and there only remained the human body serving as an organ or instrument of God.

Such, if we may credit the author of a curious book

upon heresies that was discovered some years ago, and is known by the name of the *Philosophoumena* of Hippolytus, was the doctrine of a Bishop of Rome, Callistus (218—223), who owed his election, through the means of a numerous and influential party, to his lax principles and his Unitarian opinions. It appears, according to this book, that the Unitarian tendency was still very strong in Rome at the commencement of the third century. Bishop Zephyrinus, the predecessor of Callistus, was an undisguised and simple Patripassionist, who, to avoid falling into ditheism, which he held in horror, wished, as he said, "to know only one God, Jesus Christ, one only God who was born, and who suffered." Callistus, with more subtilty, spoke of the Father and the Son as two modes, two manners of being of one sole God, of one only and the same Spirit, the Father being this God invisible, and the Son the same God visible; so that the Father had not exactly suffered, but had sympathized in suffering with the Son—a mere empty distinction, without any real meaning.*

It was from some disciples of a famous oriental Unitarian, Noetus of Smyrna, who died towards 230, that Callistus had imbibed these repulsive ideas. Noetus appears to have leaned strongly to the speculative idea

---

* May I be permitted to refer those who wish to know more about this strange contention, of which the Church of Rome was the theatre in the third century, to my article entitled *Saint Hippolyte et le Pape Calliste*, in the *Revue des Deux Mondes* for June 15, 1865 ?

of the contrary manifestations of the same identical being, applying this to the Deity; so that, as he affirmed, God may thus be at once visible and invisible, mortal and immortal, Son and Father. He found in Sabellius, a presbyter of Ptolemais (250—260), a successor who amplified and completed the system, and gave to it his name.

Sabellius did not exactly reject the idea of the Word, with which no system, it would seem, could now dispense. He only modified it so as to make it a part of his speculative theory of the Divine essence. Instead of seeing in the Word a divine person proceeding at a given moment from the bosom of God the Father, in order to serve as a medium between Him and created things, Sabellius conceived of it as an intra-divine movement, impelling the unity, or the monad, to unfold itself into a triad. God therefore, by means of the Word, becomes successively Father, Son, and Holy Spirit. These three names signify, not three distinct personal beings, but three aspects or modes ($\pi\rho\acute{o}\sigma\omega\pi\alpha$) of the Deity, corresponding to as many periods in history. The Father has to do with the period of the Law, the Son with that of the Gospel, the Spirit with that of the Church. But when God revealed himself as the Son, the Father returned to the monad; and in the same way, when he revealed himself as Spirit, the Son was re-absorbed in God.* It is by no means clear in what manner

---

* This abstract of the system of Sabellius differs considerably from those usually given of it. The Fathers, and those historians who have followed

Sabellius conceived the relation of the person of Jesus with the mode of the Divine existence designated by the name of Son. The speculative tendency of his system would lead him to pay chief attention to general ideas, and but little to facts and persons. The life of God, regarded as a matter of fact, was confounded, according to his view, with the history of the world; whilst the man Jesus could be logically only the individual manifestation of the God-Son, as the whole body of religious beliefs was the collective manifestation of the God-Spirit. A manifest tendency to pantheism characterizes this entire conception of things, and its most learned adversaries have not failed to bring against it the reproach of its affinities with Heraclitus and the Stoic School. But to the common view, Sabellianism mostly appeared as simply the doctrine which denied the distinction of persons in God, putting, in place of this, modalism, or modes of being; and it became from that time a generic name for all theories of the Divine existence which proceeded upon this kind of explanation. Thus all those theologians or philosophers, even though they may not be aware of it, fall into the Sabellian heresy, who imagine that the Trinity can be reconciled with human reason

them, have erroneously confounded the Sabellian monad, the as yet indeterminate divine unity, with the Father, as if it were the Father who became sometimes Son, and sometimes Holy Spirit. We owe to the illustrious Dr. F. C. Baur the definitive elucidation of the authentic Sabellian theory. Gieseler, *Kirchengesch.* i. p. 298, 4th edition, gives an excellent *catena* of the passages in the Fathers relating to Sabellianism.

by comparing the three divine persons with the three qualifications of *father*, *husband*, and *son*, which may be combined in one man; or, again, with the three fundamental powers of the human mind—*knowledge*, *love*, and *will*. The Trinity declares the distinct existence of three persons in one God, and not of three qualities or faculties belonging to one single person.

This Unitarianism, which started from the idea of the strict unity of God, conceivable under two forms, the one rude and popular, the other metaphysical, was not alone in its attempt to withstand the advancing ditheism. There was also a Unitarianism very similar to that prevailing in our own day in the Protestant churches, which rather takes its stand upon the real historical humanity of Jesus, and then asserts his spiritual union with the Deity. Theodotus and Artemon, at the end of the second century, preached openly in the Church at Rome the necessity of holding firmly to the Christ of the three first Gospels, to the man Jesus fully inspired by the Holy Spirit; and their adherents maintained that until the installation of Zephyrinus in the episcopal chair of Rome, a little before 200, the faith of the Christian community of the imperial city had not differed from theirs. The book of Hermas, so much of it as we have yet seen, shows that this claim has more historical foundation than we should at first have been disposed to believe, while it is indirectly confirmed by the *Philosophoumena* of Hippolytus.

At the other extremity of the Christian world, Bishop Beryllus, of Bostra in Arabia, denied the personal preexistence of Jesus, and made his **divine** character to consist in his submission to the influence of the Spirit of God. **But** it was, above all, the brilliant Bishop of Antioch, Paul of Samosata, who, from the year 260, **raised this** rational Unitarianism to the lofty position of a philosophical theory, and became, in connection with this branch of the *monarchical* tendency, what Sabellius had been for the one preceding. Christ, said he, is truly a man, but a man become divine, deified ($\theta\epsilon o\pi o\iota\eta\theta\epsilon\acute{\iota}s$). In what way? By his religious and moral perfection. Paul of Samosata could also thus appropriate the idea of the Word, not, however, attributing personality to it, in order to avoid ditheism. The Word, or Logos, was, according to him, in God as well as in man, the thinking principle which revealed itself in the creation, and which elevated the reason and the will of every man towards God. It is by virtue of this action of the Word, exercised in a super-excellent manner, that Jesus of Nazareth has become the Man-God; in other words, the man perfectly united **to** God, and in whom God reveals him**self** to save the **human** race.

The history of Paul of Samosata was a most extraordinary one. He was not only Bishop of the important church of Antioch, but also a civil magistrate, *ducenarius procurator*, that is, treasurer; and **the** liberal use he **made of his riches, together** with his affability and his remarkable talent as a preacher, had rendered him very popular in the Syrian metropolis, which was by this time almost entirely Christian. It may be that his more secular than clerical mode of life, his rationalizing tendency, and the little value which such a man would attach to bigoted forms, might have occasionally led him to some indiscretions in the contrary direction. But it is indisputable that the malevolence of his episcopal brethren made them very ready to listen to any pious denunciations tending to defame his character.* Hatred and calumny set violently against him. After long debates, he was deposed, in 269, by a Council assembled at Antioch, the members of which thought it necessary—so uncommon at that time was the deposition of a bishop for erroneous doctrine upon the person of Jesus—to blacken his reputation, in order to justify the decision. The Christian inhabitants of Antioch, who were ardently attached to their Unitarian bishop,

---

* Comp. Euseb. *Hist. Eccles.* vii. 27—30. Gieseler, *Kirchengesch.* i. p. 301, has collected the principal passages which define the doctrine of Paul of Samosata. In the circular letter of the bishops assembled at Antioch, which Eusebius gives at length, may be seen how active and malignant was the *odium theologicum* against Paul. One strange fact is that the Council, to avoid the appearance of falling into Sabellianism while condemning the doctrine of Paul, decreed that "the Son was not *consubstantial* (ὁμοούσιος) with the Father," that is to say, it condemned the expression which was to serve fifty years later to define the orthodoxy of Nicæa. It is curious to read the incredible subtilties by which Athanasius and the orthodox theologians strove to remove this stumbling-block from the history of a dogma which they desired to represent as having been the invariable doctrine of the Church.

refused to obey the Council, and still kept him for nearly three years at their head—a fact inconceivable if the accusations made against him by his enemies had had any good foundation. He was protected also by Queen **Zenobia**, then at the height of her power, who sympathized with his theological views. The **turn** that political events took was fatal to Paul. Zenobia was defeated in the war waged against her by the Emperor Aurelian, and though little inclined to favour the Christians, he was entreated by the Syrian bishops to enforce the decree of the Council. This was in 272, forty years before the accession of Constantine. The Church was already a power which the Empire must take into account. Aurelian, who had no desire to meddle with a dispute the merits of which he did not understand, settled the question on political grounds. He exiled from Antioch the favourite of the vanquished **Queen**, and declared that he would not allow any bishop in the **city who was not in harmony with the** bishops of Rome and Italy, **that is, with those** whom he was sure of having always under his control. Paul of Samosata was obliged to yield **to the** secular power, and he died in obscurity. There still **continued**, however, though **possessing** little influence, a *Samosatian*, or *Paulianist* party, until the end of the fourth century.*

Paul of Samosata closes the series of the great Uni-

---

* For fuller information, see the article entitled *Paul de Samosate et Zénobie* in the *Revue des Deux Mondes* for May 1st, 1868.

tarians of the third century. His Unitarianism, notwithstanding its intrinsic worth and its solid historical basis, could not but have failed. The current of thought was not in the direction of rationalism. More than ever was the growing prestige of Christianity, in the popular opinion, reflected upon the person of the Christ; and everything that appeared to touch his glory, by refusing to him any title of superiority whatsoever, was sure to be distasteful to the feelings of the majority of Christians. Sabellianism, as vulgarly conceived, so depreciated the Divine perfection that common sense sufficed to refute it; while as maintained in the metaphysical region in which it had been systematized by him to whom it owed its name, it was no longer understood. In neither of the two forms did it sufficiently exalt the person of Jesus: it was not he that was God; his person was but a temporary instrument, a mere accident of the Divine existence. But the spirit of the mass of Christians was well represented by the majority of the bishops, as it was constantly recruited from them by the direct or indirect choice of the churches; and it may be affirmed that, at the end of the third century, the doctrine of the Word, of the secondary god become man in Jesus Christ, which first appeared in the second century in Justin Martyr and the fourth Evangelist, and was adopted and developed by Tertullian, Clement, and Origen, reigned undisputed in the Church.

CHAPTER V.

ATHANASIUS AND ARIUS.

The pre-existence, the superhuman origin, and the relative divinity of Jesus, are thus integral parts of the doctrine which was considered orthodox at the end of the third century. But there was still more than one step to climb ere the Christian sentiment could attain complete satisfaction. The ascension of Christ towards the godhead had not yet reached its term. The Son was god, but subordinate, not yet God in the proper sense. In dealing with these contradictory ideas, the minds of men, according to their personal prepossessions, either inclined to lay great stress upon the subordination of the Son, in order to keep as close as possible to the facts of the Gospel history, or they dwelt strongly upon his divinity, in order to satisfy an ardent piety, which felt as if it could not exalt Christ too highly. From this variation of tendencies sprang two doctrines, which contended together until one should have destroyed the other,—the doctrine of Arius, and that of Athanasius. In reality, though under other forms, it was a renewal of the struggle between rationalism and mysticism. On one side was the critical, distrustful spirit that is afraid of the illusions of feeling given up solely to its own inspiratious, and seeks to guard itself against them : on the other were the intuitions of feeling accepted directly as pure truth, and only calling in the aid of knowledge and reasoning to plead a cause already decided. This conflict belongs to all ages, but seldom have the two powers entered upon a more obstinate engagement, and on a more limited arena. The destinies of the Church were determined for ten centuries by the issue of the struggle.

This struggle was very near the point of breaking forth before Arius and Athanasius came upon the scene. Bishop Dionysius of Alexandria, when engaged in a controversy with the Sabellian bishops of Lybia, had already laid stress upon the inferiority of the Son, so far as to deny his eternity, and formally to rank him amongst creatures ($\pi o\iota \acute{\eta} \mu a \tau a$). This was already Arianism complete. Bishop Dionysius of Rome (259—269), who had, besides, other grievances against his colleague of Alexandria, discovered in the expression *creature* an error insulting to the majesty of the Son, and wrote a reply which left scarcely anything remaining of the subordination until now so carefully maintained. Dionysius of Alexandria tried to soften the meaning of his expressions, and his peaceable disposition prevented the quarrel from extending. But it was easy to see that this temporary discord between the two was only the threatening of a storm which would break out sooner or later in the whole Christian Church. There were already plain indications of a marked difference between the East and the West on the subject of Christology.

The West was little given to philosophical speculations; it was much more attracted towards practical questions and matters of discipline. And while in the West the ascendency of the bishops of Rome was acknowledged everywhere, except occasionally in Africa, the Roman see, for its own part, viewing every problem, as it did, from the ecclesiastical rather than the dogmatic side, was thereby induced to prefer the views which were supported by the Christian sentiment of the multitude, and scarcely concerned itself at all with the difficulties which minds trained to philosophical discussion might feel in admitting them. It was therefore predisposed to pronounce in favour of whatever brought the divinity of Jesus Christ nearer to that absolute perfection which was the secret wish of the Christian body. The East, on the contrary, enamoured of metaphysical questions, eager for controversies, and having various centres of influence—Alexandria, Ephesus, Antioch, Jerusalem, and a little later Constantinople—was destined to be the theatre of the great theological debates. And it became, in consequence, the interest of the conflicting parties in the East always to secure, as far as possible, the support of the Roman see, which could throw into the scale all the weight of the Western Church.

At the same period the Church gained at length the supreme object of its ambition. It was about to become the ally, if not indeed the chief institution, of the Empire. Although at the beginning of the fourth century still in its minority, it was the sole living and resistant force in the midst of the old world which was falling into decay. Constantine, with the penetration of a true political genius, had early perceived this,—a fact which explains, much better than any strong religious convictions of his own, the increasing favour which he showed to the Church, or rather to the heads of the Church. What especially attracted his administrative and absolutist turn of mind, was the episcopal constitution, by that time completely formed, which concentrated the great body of Christendom in some hundreds of bishops, themselves grouped around five or six eminent members of the episcopate, so that whoever could control these last would be master of the whole.* By allying himself with the Church—doing it cautiously, however, in order to relieve the abruptness of the change to the eye of the majority, to whom it was otherwise very much a matter of indifference—the Emperor, who possessed already the rights of the pagan chief Pontificate, would easily become the real head of the Christian community, and would thus rule over the souls as well as the bodies of all. The bishops were dazzled and fascinated.

---

* Something like this must have been in the mind of the First Consul at the time of the negociations respecting the Concordat, when he paid so little regard to the guarantees which the constitution of the Gallic clergy secured to the inferior priests against episcopal tyranny.

Emerging from a precarious position, having been but just before outside the pale of law, they became suddenly the object of imperial favours. They yielded blindly to the temptation, and from the time of Constantine to the fall of the Empire a new element, namely the will of the Emperor, must be included among the causes which co-operated in the formation of Christian dogma. Orthodoxy and heresy vied with each other in courting them. A few highminded individual men alone succeeded in preserving their independence: neither party, taken as a whole, had any right to upbraid the other with its servility.

Antioch, the ancient church of the Unitarian Paul of Samosata, had been drawn again into the current of Catholicity, but it continued still to be a focus of liberalism and religious science. This character was maintained by a very celebrated school of exegesis, in which the rules of grammar and the lessons of history were applied to the interpretation of the sacred writings, instead of arbitrary allegory, as at Alexandria, or stereotyped tradition, as at Rome. A certain religious moderation and a spirit of independent opinion would necessarily arise from such a training, and in point of fact the disciples of the school of Antioch, although belonging to very diverse parties, all bear an unmistakable family likeness.

Amongst them, at the beginning of the fourth century, was a student of the name of Arius, who, on leaving

Syria, had been appointed presbyter, or pastor, of a parish in Alexandria. The strictness of his morals, his oratorical talents, and the pains he took in instructing the lower classes, gained for him the esteem and affection of the Christians of the city. It is not improbable that the influence of the presbyter, and the possibly unconscious jealousy with which he inspired Alexander, his bishop, had something to do with the origin of the controversy. It was at Alexandria, moreover, that the episcopate had the greatest difficulty in imposing its authority upon the presbytery, which had still a vivid remembrance of the ancient equality of all the pastors. Arius had already taken an active part in ecclesiastical contests in Syria. His was one of those minds which are more lucid than comprehensive, in which predominates, side by side with a keen sense of duty, a rigid though not profound logic that keeps straight onwards within the limits to which its free movement is restricted. He had brought with him from Antioch a very strong taste for dialectic deduction, a minute acquaintance with the Christian literature of the early centuries, and a marked antipathy to Sabellianism. The theory of the personal Logos was in his opinion, as in that of most of his contemporaries, a settled matter; but he feared the tendency which, by increasingly diminishing the difference between the Son and the Father, was forcing opinion into the necessary alternative of the Sabellian modalism, or of ditheism; and he inclined in consequence towards the express definition of the inferiority of the Son in order to keep clear of this double danger.

The Son, he said, is subordinate to the Father; upon this point every one is agreed. But if the Son is subordinate to the Father, he is not absolutely God; he has not all that the Father has; in other words, he is not equal to the Father. Not being equal, he is not of the same substance as the Father; for if he were, that substance being perfect, he would himself be perfect, and there would be two Gods equal in everything, which is polytheism and an absurdity. On the other hand, besides the One uncreated Being, there can be only created beings, that is, beings born in time, brought by God out of nothing (ἐξ οὐκ ὄντων). The Son, therefore, is not eternal: he is a creature; the first and most excellent of creatures, by whose instrumentality God created all others, but still a creature. If he is spoken of as "made," "begotten," or "formed," these expressions are of small importance; they amount simply to this, that he has not in himself the principle of his own existence, which constitutes precisely the difference between created beings and the Uncreated Being. In a word, the Son is not co-essential nor consubstantial with the Father (οὐκ ὁμοούσιος); he did not exist from all eternity; there was a time when he was not (ἦν ποτε ὅτε οὐκ ἦν). These two negations were the distinguishing device of the doctrine which soon came to bear the name of Arianism.

In reality, Arius, whose character and doctrine have been unjustly vilified by orthodox historians, was in the wrong only in stating with a somewhat uncompromising precision the ecclesiastical doctrine that had been previously in common acceptance. The defects of his system were due much more to the tradition of his time than to himself. The New Testament, the discrepancies of which in regard to doctrine were now no longer discerned, taught from beginning to end, even in the fourth Gospel, the inferiority of the Son. All the writers prior to the fourth century, with the sole exception of the Sabellians, shared this view, which, besides, formed an integral part of the theory of the Word, and appeared to them necessary to the preservation of Monotheism. Origen, again, the great doctor of Alexandria, had been much bolder than Arius, if his system be regarded as a whole. And when Arius said, "there was a time when the Son was not," did he express himself differently from Tertullian, one of the authors of the traditional doctrine? And when he denied the Homoousia, or consubstantiality of the Son with the Father, could he not invoke in his favour the express decree of that Council of Antioch which had excommunicated at the same time Paul of Samosata and Sabellius?

All this is unquestionable, at least for one who studies without orthodox prejudice the history of the first centuries. But in the historical appreciation of a doctrinal tradition it is necessary to distinguish the tendency which that tradition follows, from the successive momenta or crises of development in which it finds expression. The misfortune of Arius was, that, supported as he evidently was by the authority of the earlier ecclesiastical writers, he was nevertheless setting himself in opposition to the ascending current of Christian ideas, which, from the beginning, had never ceased to approximate Jesus ever more nearly to God. The strength of his opponents, on the contrary, consisted in their accordance with this direction, which from the first the Christian sentiment had taken. Arius had to struggle against the rising tide; they were supported by it.

Arius's bishop, Alexander, after some hesitation, at length considered that the moment for attack had arrived. In 321, a Council which was held under his presidency at Alexandria deposed and excommunicated the refractory presbyter. The spirit of the episcopal order could not allow that a presbyter might be right in opposition to his bishop, and this original sin obtruded itself from first to last to the disadvantage of Arianism. Arius, not submitting to his defeat, sought for allies among the bishops of the East, his old friends at Antioch, amongst whom he had reason to expect greater sympathy with his views. Many of them, in fact, and amongst others Eusebius, the bishop of Nicomedia, and the celebrated historian, Eusebius of Cæsarea, interposed in his favour, as much at least as was possible without compromising the prestige of episcopal authority. They tried, above all things, to hush up the difference; but this effort in favour of peace did not succeed. The controversy grew more bitter, and spread everywhere. Constantine was greatly annoyed with a quarrel the importance of which he did not understand, and which gave a check to his project of unification. After having tried in vain to impose silence on the two parties, there being also other points in dispute which required settling, he thought it best to summon the whole body of bishops, to unite for the first time in an *Œcumenical Council* at Nicæa in Bythinia, close to Nicomedia, where he then resided. He was, besides, glad to seize this opportunity of bringing around him all the bishops, fully expecting that he could influence them sufficiently to lay the foundation of a Christian supreme pontificate which would add a new lustre to the imperial authority.

Catholic historians have always been much embarrassed to account for the singularly uninfluential part taken by the Roman See in these first great sessions of the Christian Church. They have pretended, for example, that Sylvester, a person of very little note, but who was then the bishop of Rome, convoked the Council through the channel of the imperial authority, and was represented at Nicæa by legates who presided in his name. All this is mere imagination. There is not the least trace of it either in contemporary documents, or in the acts of the Council. The fact is, that Constantine of his own accord summoned the meeting of the Council, and delegated the presidency of it to Bishop Hosius of Cordova who was at the time in great favour at his court, and whom he appointed to this important office to prevent the rivalries of the Eastern bishops. In the year 325, three hundred and eighteen bishops, a large majority of whom were from the East, responded to the imperial summons.

Three parties were in fact represented at Nicæa. We have just seen in what Arianism consisted. It was the natural result of the contest once begun, that the opponents of Arius had formulated their views of the divinity of Jesus Christ in such a manner as to bring him as near to deity as Arius had sought to distinguish him from it. Their opinion was defended before the Council by an archdeacon of Alexandria named Athanasius, who soon became the leading champion of the absolute divinity of Jesus. Athanasius ranks in history along with Augustine and Thomas Aquinas, as one of the three great names of orthodoxy. Passionately devoted to his theology, a profound thinker, though a poor interpreter of Scripture; unyielding himself, but skilful in the management of others, and not unwilling, when policy required it, to make concessions not vitally affecting the ultimate victorious issue; intolerant, yet able to bear with courage and dignity the intolerance of the opposite party; delighted if he could oppose the errors of his adversaries with the aid of the secular authorities, although himself incapable of conforming his opinions to the will of any earthly power—Athanasius, the mystic and the subtile logician, stands out before the eyes of the modern historian as one of those imposing figures that we admire but do not love. With men of this stamp, the craving for rule puts out of sight the sympathetic aspects of their character; and when the ideas identified with their names have grown out of date, we require to remind ourselves of the duty of historical justice in order not to be unfair towards them.

Athanasius, and those who agreed with him, had set forth counter propositions to those of the Arians. The *Homoousia*, the consubstantiality of the Son and the Father, was especially prized by them as expressing, or necessarily implying, all that Arius disputed. The Word, or the Son, they said, is of the same substance as the Father: to deny this would be to lower him to the rank of a creature, and to do violence to Christian feeling. Being of the same substance, he is eternal, having always existed as a personal and distinct being in the presence of God the Father, from whom he becomes separated by virtue of a mysterious generation. The distinction, which had been formerly held so essential, of the Word as internal and impersonal, from the Word emitted, and so become personal, had in this view no longer any meaning, or at least it was only an abstract, logical distinction, without objective reality. There was no further ground for affirming a real subordination of the Son to the Father, excepting that the

Father was the original cause of the being of the Son. Their equality in dignity, glory, power, and perfection, was therefore implied in the Homoousia; while the unity of the substance possessed in common by the Father and the Son was considered sufficient to preserve the truth of Monotheism.

But the majority of the Council were at heart neither with Arius, whose formulas were too incisive to please them, nor with Athanasius, whom they accused of innovation. They would have preferred a middle course, maintaining the traditional idea of the subordination of the Son to the Father, while ascribing to the Son as much of divine attributes as they could without openly passing this limit. However inconsistent this middle course might be, they would willingly have adopted a confession of faith so elastic that the Arians might fairly have accepted it. Eusebius of Cæsarea drew up such a confession, and almost succeeded in having it passed. But the adversaries of Arius having pointed out to Constantine that equivocal expressions would not decide the difference, and that the Council would fail in its object if it left things as they were, he gave the bishops to understand that they must arrive at a clear decision if they wished to please him. He was, besides, prejudiced against the presbyter Arius, who had committed the grave fault of allowing himself to dispute with his bishop. What would be the consequence if all the presbyters should take a similar liberty? Learning, therefore, that the expression Homoousia, which had been half agreed to by the majority, would be summarily rejected by the Arians, he insisted peremptorily upon its adoption. The majority submitted to the official pressure, and declared themselves ready to decree the Homoousia, or the consubstantiality of the Father and the Son, the more willingly because Eusebius had represented to them that this scholastic term could be understood legitimately of the "analogy" or "resemblance" between the essence of the Son and that of the Father, without implying their perfect equality. There were, however, seventeen bishops, determined Arians, who refused their adhesion, but they nearly all soon yielded to the seductions and threats of the Emperor. Arius, Theonas, the bishop of Lybia, and Secundus, the bishop of Ptolemais, had alone the signal honour of inaugurating the resistance of the Christian conscience to that pressure of the temporal power which has perverted more characters than have been driven to apostasy by the most cruel persecutions. They paid the penalty of their independence in their deposition and exile to Illyria. Eusebius of Nicomedia and Theognis of Nicæa consented to subscribe to the Confession of Nicæa, but not to the anathemas at its close. They also fell into disgrace, and were banished to Gaul. Their names ought to be inscribed in letters of gold on the page of history.

The following is the Creed which was decided upon

at Nicæa. It is constructed, as will be seen, upon the basis of the primitive trilogy:

"We believe in one only God, the Father Almighty, Author of all things visible and invisible:

"And in one only Lord, Jesus Christ, the Son of God, only begotten of the Father, that is to say, **of the substance of the Father**; God of God; Light of Light; **True God of True God**; begotten **and** not created; consubstantial (ὁμοούσιον) with the Father: by whom all things **are, as** well in heaven as on earth; who came down for **us men and** for our salvation; who was incarnate and **became man**; who suffered; who was raised the third day, and ascended into heaven; who will come again to judge the living and the **dead**:

"And in the Holy Spirit.

"As to those who say, *There was a time when he was not;* and *before he was begotten he was not;* and *he was made out of nothing;* or who pretend that the Son of God **is of** another essence or substance, that he is created, or mutable, or alterable,—the Catholic Apostolic Church anathematizes them."

Athanasius and his party triumphed. The Homoousia became henceforth law in the Church. Yet this victory **was** still rather apparent than real. Constantine had forced the position. Homoousia **was** interpreted in the sense proposed by Eusebius of Cæsarea. To speak correctly, what was understood by it was only Homoiousia (ὁμοιούσια), a resemblance rather than an identity of substance; enough to separate the Son from all creatures, not enough to determine his absolute divinity. Arianism, which had been overcome by the imperial will more than by the free judgment of the bishops, retained its power in the churches. Many influential and popular presbyters openly declared their Arian sympathies. Arianism took the lead in the first missions amongst the Germanic tribes. It had even its partisans at court, the Princess Constantia, the sister of the Emperor, being amongst them. Scarcely had two years passed before Constantine discovered, as he thought, that, from defect of learning in theology, he had taken a false step in the interest of the general peace. Perhaps he perceived also, with some alarm, that he had set a dangerous precedent by too closely implicating the imperial authority with the settlement of a point of metaphysical doctrine. The fact is certain that he recalled Arius from exile in the year 328, only demanding from him a confession of faith conceived in such general terms that he could have no reason for refusing.* The Emperor then desired that he should be reinstated in his office at Alexandria. But Athanasius, who had lately become the bishop of that

* Party spirit and hatred have invented the charge against Arius that he falsely led the Emperor to believe that he was signing the Nicene Creed, whilst he was doing nothing of the kind. Neander, although little favourable to Arius, whose somewhat sharp clearness accorded little with his character of mind, has well shown the groundlessness of this accusation. Besides, at that period Constantine scarcely held to the Nicene Creed, and he certainly regretted having displayed so much energy in securing its adoption.

city, positively refused to admit his former opponent amongst the presbyters of his diocese, notwithstanding that he had just been formally welcomed back into the ranks of the Christian clergy by a synod which had assembled at Jerusalem to consecrate the Church of the Holy Sepulchre. Warm debates followed this refusal, the issue of which was that Athanasius in his turn was forced to go into exile. Arius was about to make his triumphal re-entry into the Church of Constantinople, much against the will of the bishop of the new capital, who was a warm advocate of the *homoousian* doctrine, when he was carried off by a sudden attack of internal disease. His enemies saw in this sudden death a divine punishment, while his friends believed that a crime had been skilfully perpetrated. The truth respecting this matter will never be known. The death of Arius may possibly have been quite natural, but it occurred so exactly at the right moment that suspicion is natural also.*

It was clearly seen how factitious, or, at the very

---

* We need scarcely say that these suspicions could not touch either the orthodox party as a whole, or any of its leaders. But who does not know how far fanaticism can go in the lower ranks of a religious party? Bishop Alexander of Constantinople, according to the strongly anti-Arian historian Socrates, would seem to have addressed a prayer to Heaven, which may be summed up thus: "Oh God, call me from this world, or cause this Arius to die!" This prayer was not a silent one, or it could not have been reported (Socrates, *Hist. Eccles.* i. 25). Can we be sure that no person came to the conclusion that the death of this holy bishop must be averted, and that it would be a pious work to aid the divine wisdom in deciding for the latter alternative of this notable dilemma?

least, premature, had been the victory of the Athanasian party at Nicæa, so soon as by the turn of imperial favour the majority of the Eastern bishops were at liberty to express their true sentiments. People did not believe at that period in the infallibility of councils. The West alone remained firm in adhesion to the faith of Nicæa. Constantine dying in 337, the empire was divided between his two sons, Constans ruling in the West, and Constantius in the East. Constans was Catholic. Constantius, though not Arian, was of that intermediate shade of opinion called *semi-Arian*, or *Eusebian*, after its chief representative, Eusebius of Nicomedia. He had been restored to favour by Constantine, and under his successor was more powerful than ever, having become, since 338, the bishop of Constantinople. Each of the two emperors professed, in fact, precisely the belief which the majority of the Christian people of his own division of the empire preferred.

In 341, a numerously attended Council was held at Antioch, which tried to settle the somewhat fluctuating views of this Eusebian or semi-Arian party, by avoiding the word *homoousia*, while exalting as much as possible the person of the Son. But new and bitter controversies followed, new schisms, new arbitrary interventions of the temporal power. In 347, Constantius and Constans, in the interest of peace, convoked an Œcumenical Council at Sardica in Mœsia; but it was attended only by the party of the West, that of the East assembling at Philippopolis, while both sides kept firm to their own opinions.

It would be impossible, without indefinitely prolonging a narration already very complicated, to notice all the changing issues of this painful conflict, in which the Christian Church, on the eve of the barbarian invasions, consumed its best strength in the discussion of inextricable subtilties. The semi-Arians reproached the Athanasians with falling necessarily into Sabellianism by assimilating the Son to the Father to such a degree that they could only be regarded logically as two modes of the same Divine subsistence. Marcellus of Ancyra, and his pupil Photinus of Sirmium, the latter especially, struck upon that rock which Athanasius, with all his skill, had hardly been able to avoid. Photinianism was condemned by the second Council of Antioch in 345, the Council of Milan in 347, and the Council of Sirmium in 351. This doctrine was a revival of the old Unitarianism, since it distinguished the divine Word from the personal Son of God, reserving this name for the incarnate Word, in other words for the man Jesus, the organ of the Word.

Meanwhile, Constans had died in 350. Constantius, having overcome Maxentius, reigned alone from 353, and endeavoured to give predominance in the West to the semi-Arianism which already prevailed in the East. The same imperial pressure which had been brought to bear upon the Council of Nicæa with the purpose of procuring the condemnation of Arius, was now brought to bear upon the Councils of Arles (353) and Milan (355), in order to obtain the condemnation of Athanasius. The recalcitrant bishops were deposed and banished; amongst others, Lucifer of Cagliari, Hilary of Poitiers, and Pope Liberius.

The world was thus in an official sense semi-Arian, being perhaps less surprised with its position than was St. Hilary, who affirms somewhere that " the world was astounded thereat." In reality, semi-Arianism was a malleable, vaguely defined form of belief, under shelter of which Arianism was reaping a rich harvest. Men of talent, as, for instance, Aëtius of Antioch, Eunomius of Cappadocia, and Acacius of Cæsarea, feared not to oppose as energetically the *homoiousia*,* that is, the similarity of the substances, as the *homoousia*, or their identity. With them the latent rationalism of the Arian tendency came out into distinct and vigorous life, and threatened to extend to many other points of ecclesiastical doctrine. Constantius was semi-Arian, but he wished to set the Church at peace; and in the hope of extending even over the true Arians the wide mantle of ecclesiastical

---

* The term ὁμοιούσιος τῷ πατρί served as a distinctive mark to the semi-Arian party, who regretted more than ever the adoption of ὁμοούσιος at Nicæa. It could therefore be said with truth that at that moment the peace of the world and of the Church depended upon an ι. In reality this iota was but the sharp point of an imposing pyramid of facts, speculations, and sentiments, which represented at the time the first power in the world.

unity, he contrived that the second Council of Sirmium (357) should draw up a formula general enough to satisfy everybody. As usually happens in such cases, no one was content. Semi-Arianism maintained its *homoiousia* at the Council of Ancyra (358); whereupon a third Council of Sirmium, held the same year, rejected the confession of faith promulgated by the second, and adhered to the anathemas launched at Ancyra.* Then a new turn of expression was tried. It was proposed to acknowledge the Son as "like (ὅμοιος) the Father in all things, in such manner as the Holy Scriptures speak and teach;" and a Council of the West held at Rimini, and one of the East at Seleucia (359),† after much laboured debating, adopted this formula of agreement, which did not, however, reconcile any of the contending parties. Two years afterwards Constantius died, leaving his memory burdened with a reputation for intolerance, which he only so far deserved that, wishing to give peace to the Church at any price, he committed the error of using his power, as his father had done before

---

* It was on this occasion that Pope Liberius, being tired of exile and desirous of regaining his episcopal see, was so weak as to give in his adhesion in writing to two semi-Arian confessions. A Gallican of those times would of course have been semi-Arian, since the heresy had on its side the Pope and the Council.

† The Council of Rimini was attended by four hundred bishops, of whom eighty were pure Arians; that of Seleucia by a hundred and sixty, of whom a hundred and five were semi-Arians, and the rest Athanasians. I borrow these figures from the article *Arianismus* in the *Theologische Encyclopädie* of Herzog.

him, to seduce the weak and to exile men of independence of character, who appeared to him the causers of trouble and incorrigible mischief-makers.

The interference of the political power with the affairs of the Church ceased for a time. Julian (361—363) tried to convert the world to his romantic polytheism, and in the mean time revoked all former edicts of banishment for religion. It was the Athanasian party, who had been the greatest sufferers in the last reign, that gained the most from this change. Their bishops, Athanasius amongst them, returned in triumph to their dioceses, where most of the Christian part of the population, being tired of the late government, received them with enthusiasm. Under Jovian, who died in 364, under Valentinian I., who died in 375, and under Gratian and Valentinian II., toleration generally prevailed. Valens, on the contrary, a zealous Arian, who was Emperor of the East from 364 to 378, wished to secure the triumph of Arianism by force. But this imperial protection, with the abuses and scandals which it produced, had the contrary effect, and only hastened its disappearance. The semi-Arian party, feeling shocked and frightened, drew nearer to the Athanasians. Three learned men, Basil the Great, Gregory of Nazianzen, and Gregory of Nyssa, though substantially more or less semi-Arian in their opinions, favoured this reconciliation. Athanasius himself advised that there should not be shown too great severity towards these new allies, if they would but accept the distinctive consecrated terms. On this condition he would not himself deny absolutely that there might be some truth in that subordination of the Son to the Father to which the semi-Arian party held with such tenacity. It should be remarked that his condescension was openly censured by some excited partisans of his own side. But Athanasius knew well what he was doing. It was evident that the great majority of the Church was won over to the doctrine of Nicæa. In vain did Valentinian II. and his mother Justina still for a time patronize Arianism in the West.* When the Spaniard Theodosius, an ardent Catholic, ascended the imperial throne, he found his own party, which was the Athanasian, rapidly gaining the ascendency; and his laws, which were far more tyrannical than the edicts of Valens, easily established the formula decreed at Nicæa as the definitive and the unchangeable orthodoxy of Christendom.

With the Germanic invasions, however, Arianism enjoyed a return of prosperity. The Goths, the Vandals, the Suevians, the Burgundians, and the Lombards, who parcelled out the empire of the West into independent kingdoms, were Arian Christians when they came upon the imperial territory, and they so remained for some time after their conquests. But Arianism was with most of them rather a matter of tradition than of deliberate

---

* Theodosius sold to him his support against the usurper Maximus at the price of the oppression of the Arians of the West.

choice. They had embraced Christianity under its Arian form, because their missionaries, among others the celebrated Ulphilas, who converted the Goths, inclined to the Arian views which were in general those of the ordinary clergy of the fourth century. It is not uninteresting, by the way, to observe that the first great conquest of Christianity beyond the Roman Empire was achieved by the heterodox, and in a heterodox spirit. But when the German Arians came to establish themselves in the heart of the ancient world, they found Arianism completely discountenanced in the community of Rome, the Roman episcopal see possessing a prestige without rival in the West, and the Roman clergy, which was very superior to their own, wholly imbued with the Athanasian doctrine. Their Arianism could not long withstand the absorbing influence of the Roman Catholicism. The Arian barbarians, with the exception of the Vandals in Africa, were generally more tolerant than the Roman emperors; but the sword of the French kings, when they had become converted to Catholic Christianity, hastened a result which was certainly inevitable. It would be a very curious study (although perhaps one very difficult, if not impossible) to trace out the secret links which connect the existence of non-Catholic communities in the south of France and on both sides of the Alps, along the line of the most distinctively heretical movements of the middle ages, with that leaven of anti-Romanism which the decline of

Arianism must have left in the countries long inhabited by the Goths, Burgundians, and Lombards.

Arianism, it must be acknowledged, was not calculated for long duration. It was, in reality, only one of the stations on the route which the Church had followed for three centuries, and which must of necessity bring it to the belief in the absolute deity of Jesus Christ. The Church did not abandon without hesitation, and even a kind of remorse, the inheritance of earlier days, but it was urged forward by the premises it had adopted. It should be remembered that Arianism was then considered as the extreme expression of theological boldness. The Unitarianism of a Paul of Samosata, the idea that the personality of Jesus was, to begin with, a human personality, and that it is from this point that we must set out in order to arrive logically at the real union of man with God, no longer found any response in the fourth century. Photinus, who appeared to return to it by way of the *homoousia*, was scarcely listened to. Nestorius, of whom we shall presently speak, was put down almost without a conflict. Arius, like Athanasius, placed the personality of Jesus outside humanity, but he refused to carry this conception to its full issue; while, again, he recoiled before the strict consequences of his view of Christ as a subordinate being. His Jesus was in truth neither man nor God.

Arianism, then, was untenable as a definitive system. But it is evident that, if it had triumphed over its adversaries, it would by degrees have inclined towards Unitarianism. This tendency was already perceptible in Eunomius. As held by its supporters in the fourth century, it elevated too far the created being whom it called the only Son, of whose worship it approved, and whose actual omnipotence it recognized, to escape the accusation of polytheism which its opponents raised against it; while they never asked themselves if, in another way, they did not equally deserve the same imputation.

Arianism, besides, was profoundly deistical. It separated the Creator from the creation by a wide gulf, and Athanasius argued successfully against it from the fact that it could not establish the real, positive union of man with God. This argument is very strong, regarded from the point of view of the religious sentiment. Man, according to Arianism, was without doubt united with the incarnate Son, but this incarnate Son was himself removed from God by the whole of that infinite distance which separates the uncreated Being from the highest of his creatures. Since the middle of the fourth century, we find that Arianism, while continuing very widely spread amongst the enlightened classes and the more thoughtful of the clergy, who were habituated to biblical studies and well acquainted with the tradition of the Church, became increasingly unpopular. It is evidently on this account that the Arian or semi-Arian Councils, in drawing up their dogmatic formulas, now confined themselves to keeping clear of any expression implying formal adhesion to the doctrine of Athanasius, while at the same time they came as near to it as they could. They appear, therefore, not to have dared openly to express their opinions.

It should be added that the Arian party, representing as it did the opposition to ecclesiastical authority and dogmatizing mysticism, was the party generally preferred by the freer minds. It was consequently the least united. For the same reason was it the most opposed to the ascetic, monkish, and superstitious customs which more and more pervaded the Church. Vigilantius, Aerius, and Jovinian, those Protestants of the fourth century, who contended with all their might against sacerdotal innovations, against prayers for the dead, against the holding of celibacy as the highest order of virtue, against the adoration of the saints, and other such practices, were all, as well as their followers, more or less Arians. But what would commend Arianism to us in these days rendered it at that period unpopular.

It has been stated that the triumph of the Athanasian dogma was chiefly owing to the monks, who from the fourth century became numerous and influential, and who set themselves up everywhere as fervent defenders of the *homoousia*. The fact shows with what eager sympathy the doctrine of Athanasius was received by the ignorant and zealous portion of the Christian community. It was indeed from this class that the monkhood of the fourth century was principally recruited, an age in which it was already easier to defend a cause by monks than by reasons.

Assuredly the doctrine of Athanasius was not less open to objections of all kinds than that of Arius. But the multitude perceived the weak side of the one, and were insensible to the faults of the other. We touch here upon the true point which decides the question, viewed as a matter of history. The generality of Christians understood nothing of the debates of the learned men who were fencing with each other about hypostases and essences, the *homoousia* and the *homoiousia*. But they understood perfectly that, in the view of the Arians Jesus was less than in that of the Athanasians. It therefore seemed to them that these were the better Christians. To secure the triumph of Arianism, a triumph which would have been, we repeat, but the first steps of a return towards the primitive Unitarianism, the Church, instead of marching on towards the sacerdotal, mystic, superstitious Catholicism of the middle ages, should have been animated throughout with the felt need and the desire of a reform in the sense of a simple return to the gospel. It would have required that the human mind should have reached the level which it was not to attain until eleven centuries later, that is, at the eve of the Reformation. Arianism was doomed to fail by the same necessity which led to the constitution of the Roman Catholicism, and our regrets at its final defeat will depend entirely upon the views we hold with regard to the necessity of that constitution of the Church. At the same time, the irremediable fall of a system which had, we may say, more than one chance of victory, shows indisputably the reality of that law to which we traced from the beginning this entire development of religious thought, namely, that, of the two parties in the struggle, the one which invariably triumphs is that which most glorifies the person of Jesus Christ.

The history of the worship of Mary offers one of the most instructive parallels to that of the deity of her Son. In our days, and in spite of the very powerful reasons which ancient Catholic orthodoxy could allege, the great majority of fervent Catholics have declared themselves in favour of the dogma of the Immaculate Conception, without very clearly understanding the point at issue, but mainly because their profound devotion to Mary finds more satisfaction in proclaiming this doctrine than in denying it. The gradual deification of Mary is following, in the Romish Church, though much more slowly, a course analogous to that pursued by the Church of the first centuries in elaborating the deity of Jesus. With almost all the Catholic writers of our days Mary is the universal mediatrix; *all power has been given to her in heaven and upon earth.* Nay, more—the serious attempt has already been made more than once in the Ultramontane camp to unite Mary in some way to the Trinity; and it will be done if Mariolatry lasts much longer.

CHAPTER VI.

THE DOGMAS OF THE TRINITY AND THE TWO NATURES.

In order not to impair clearness of narration, we have so far omitted to speak of certain correlative points, the settlement of which was imperatively required by the doctrine once arrived at of the absolute divinity of Jesus Christ, if it was to be reconciled with other requirements of the Christian faith and of Christian sentiment. These grew out of two quite legitimate considerations. First, supposing the Son no longer regarded as a being essentially subordinate to the Creator of all things, but as a divine, eternal person, of the same substance with the Father, how, without falling into Sabellianism and denying the personality of the Word, must the unity of God be conceived of? On the other hand, if the Son is God, of an essence perfect and unchangeable, like the Father, of whose essential nature he partakes, what idea must be entertained of the evangelical history and its human Christ, weeping, tempted, suffering, dying—in a word, partaking largely of the imperfections of our nature? To the first question the Christian theology replied by the dogma of the Trinity, which teaches the existence of three persons in one divine nature; and to the second by the dogma of the two natures, which teaches the co-existence of the human nature and the divine nature in one single person, Jesus Christ. But it was not without prolonged debates that Christendom, or rather its learned men—for the people certainly now understood nothing about it—at last agreed as to what was to be regarded as the doctrine of the Church on these two obscure points.

It will be remembered that, from the commencement of the second century, the objects of Christian faith were commonly summed up in the form of a trilogy, of the Father, the Son, and the Holy Spirit. This formula, mysterious in character and incomprehensible to the uninitiated, suited admirably an association, the scattered groups of which were so frequently compelled to establish themselves in the position of secret societies. It was not the only formula which was adopted under the kind of free-masonry to which the Christians of the early centuries so often had recourse, whether as a precaution against persecuting powers, or perhaps from the taste for mysteries which prevailed at the time. Adopted in the second century as a baptismal formula, this trilogy served as a foundation to the *rule of faith* which we find obtaining, with numerous particular differences in form, in most of the Catholic communities at the end of the century, and which, insisting upon the unity of the Creator, and the reality of the birth, sufferings, and death of Jesus, served as an antidote against the Gnostic doctrines. It was this rule of faith which grew, after undergoing some remarkable modifications, into what is now called the Apostles' Creed, or the *Credo*. We have explained how the trilogy became in the East the Triad, in the West the Trinity; though this form of expression, peculiar to the higher theology, was neither as yet popularly used, nor understood to imply the modern orthodox Trinitarian doctrine. And, further, it will be remembered how fluctuating opinion still was upon the third term, the Holy Spirit.

It was impossible that this state of things should continue. The divinity of Jesus Christ, thus become absolute, required a somewhat better-framed theory of the Trinity than the Divinity with two hands of Irenæus, or than even the *Distributive Economy* of Tertullian. The Son distinct from the Father, from whom he draws his being, but otherwise equal with the Father, constituted a kind of antithesis to him, a sort of intra-divine opposition, which required its synthesis to complete the idea. But the triple form pleases the human mind. It is the harmony which unites discords; it is the conclusion of the syllogism; it is unity disengaging itself from multiplicity; the medium of transition uniting separate terms; the point of reconcilement of the two paradoxical statements which form an antinomy. It readily suggests, therefore, the feeling of something completed, of the harmonious, the perfect; and it is not surprising that the number three should always and everywhere have occupied an important position in religious symbolism. A mystic number, it is also, or at least it marks, the number of the dialectic rhythm; and for this reason it has been in favour with the metaphysicians of every age from Pythagoras to Hegel. We do not at all mean to say that this quality of the number three has originated the belief in the Trinity; but we do in this way explain the kind of instinctive attraction that this doctrine, once built upon premises considered incontrovertible, possessed for the mind, and the facility with which transcendental speculation, mysticism, and popular faith, vied with each other in accepting it.

The Nicene Creed says nothing as yet of the Trinity, and confines itself to enunciating the ancient trilogy, Father, Son and Holy Spirit; specifying only, on the subject of the Son, the points of discussion raised by the Arian controversy. It simply affirms belief in the Holy Spirit, without declaring anything as to its nature, or its relations with the two first terms. Already, however, the words *Triad* and *Trinity* were employed to designate collectively the three divine terms; and Athanasius, in his writings against the Arians, insisted upon the impropriety of introducing a created being into the Divine Trinity. Still, many persons in his time regarded the Holy Spirit, as the Word had formerly been regarded, as a created being, subordinate to the Son, in the same manner as he was to the Father, a kind of archangel. They could even cite the formal authority of Origen in favour of this view. The Arians and semi-Arians readily inclined to this idea, which accorded with the analogy of their beliefs; whilst others, less ready to assume, without strict necessity, the existence of several Divine persons, preferred to see in it the ἐνέργεια, the operating power of God.* There were those who shrank from giving to it the name of God. Hilary of Poitiers, for example, systematically abstained from so calling it. Macedonius, the bishop of Constantinople from 342, a semi-Arian who had become almost orthodox, distinguished himself amongst those who insisted upon the inferiority of the Holy Spirit, as if he had concentrated upon this single point the leaven of Arianism which he still retained in his mind. Hence was the name of *Macedonians* given to the opponents of the deity or personality of the Holy Spirit, though it is often used also by the ancient writers, when referring to this period, to denote the semi-Arian party as a whole. Now this conception of the Holy Spirit as created and subordinate put in peril the absolute deity of the Son. Here was once more a God of second rank. It therefore appeared absolutely necessary, in order to consolidate the doctrine of Nicæa, to apply to the Holy Spirit definitions formally establishing its personality, the identity of its essence with that of the Father and of the Son, and the equal dignity which the Church should accord to it in its worship. This is what was done by the second Œcumenical Council, named the Council of Constantinople, which was convoked by Theodosius in 381 in order to

* Comp. Gregory of Nazianzen, *Orat. Theol. de Spir. Sancto*, § 5.

decree the irrevocable victory of the Athanasian doctrines. This Council re-affirmed the Nicene Creed, but added to it, on the subject of the Holy Spirit, the following declaration :

"We believe in the Holy Spirit, the Lord who gives life; who proceeds from the Father; who must be worshipped and glorified with the Father and the Son; who spoke by the prophets."

Thus was decreed the triplicity of the Divine persons. Yet the Creed of Constantinople, while beginning with a formal profession of Monotheism, says not a word of the manner in which the unity of the Deity, thus divided into three distinct persons, was to be understood; and more, in stating that the Holy Spirit proceeded from the Father, and not from the Son,* it left still hovering about a shadow of subordination of the Son and of the Holy Spirit in their relations with the Father. The Father, begetting the Son and causing the procession of the Holy Spirit, remains alone the absolute source of being and life. We can scarcely avoid seeing in this reticence of the Council a proof of the latent power

---

* The West was not slow to add habitually *Filioque*, in order to do away with this inequality, and the addition was sanctioned by the Synod of Toledo in 580. This was the origin of violent debates between the Latin and Greek Churches, the latter of which always reproached the West with having arbitrarily made this addition to the œcumenical text. Evidently the form was arbitrarily changed, but as to the sense of the alteration it is certain that the Latin Church is on this point more faithful to the spirit of the Trinitarian dogma than the Greek Church.

which semi-Arianism, though officially vanquished, still possessed in the Greek Church. The characteristic of this party from its origin had been to resign itself to the premises of its opponents, on condition that it was not obliged to concede their final conclusions.

But so great was still the diversity of opinions concealed under the common profession of the orthodox dogma, that there existed already in the Church a new form of belief, which joined to a lively sympathy with the Nicene doctrine very suspicious views respecting the person of Jesus. Apollinaris, the bishop of Laodicea, the son of a Christian writer and a great admirer of Greek literature, himself a good grammarian and an author of ability, had begun by vigorously attacking Arianism, and had gained the friendship of Athanasius. But being less absorbed with the question of the *homoousia*, he came to the conclusion that Arianism could only be vanquished by being met on the ground of historical reality. He allowed, to begin with, that the Nicene orthodoxy would end in absurdity, if, in proclaiming the deity of the Word or the Son, it arrived at the point of uniting a perfect God and a perfect man in the single person of Jesus. The idea of a God-man, which appeared to him a logical monstrosity, he did not shrink from comparing with the fabulous forms known in mythology under the name of *minotaurs* or *tragelaphs*.* Besides, said he, where man exists com-

* Grotesque animals, half goats, half stags.

plete, sin exists also (ὅπου τέλειος ἄνθρωπος, ἐκεῖ ἁμαρτία). In order to avoid the difficulty, taking his stand upon the Platonic psycholygy, which he could support by the authority of an Apostle,* and distinguishing between the *spirit*, the *soul*, and the *body* in man, he affirmed that in Jesus the soul and the body were human, and that the Word was in him what the spirit is in other men. There was, therefore, in reality but one nature in the person of Jesus, and what was human in him was only the earthly organ of the Divine Being come down upon the world.

This theory of Apollinaris attracted much attention. It denied in the most formal manner that Jesus had been truly man; and the dialectic vigour with which its author argued deprived him of the benefit of the excuses which the vagueness and indecision of former teachings on this essential point allowed to be made in apology for the ecclesiastical writers of the past. But while this view removed all real ground from the idea cherished in all ages by Christian mysticism, that in Jesus humanity has been positively united and reconciled with deity, it seemed to be strictly deducible from the doctrine decreed at Nicæa. And it was no other than a friend of the great Athanasius who developed it with such captivating clearness! Athanasius opposed Apollinaris in two of his works, but without naming him. Gregory of Nazianzen, Gregory of Nyssa, and Basil the Great,

* 1 Thess. v. 23.

attacked him without reserve, though finding themselves at times on the very verge of the idea so dangerous for orthodoxy, that there is no specific difference between the indwelling of the divine in Jesus and the same indwelling in every other man. But neither here did logic and argument decide in the last resort, any more than in the Arian controversy. The Christian sentiment of the day called for the complete and real deity of Christ, and for his real and complete humanity. Apollinaris, who had been excommunicated in 375, was definitively condemned at Constantinople in 381. He died in 390. His adherents, reduced to the position of a sect, were persecuted by the imperial authority. But notwithstanding, the essential idea of Apollinaris was afterwards revived under the name of *Monophysism*.

The Councils had decreed the faith, but not at all the relative order of its parts. In proportion as the obligatory profession of the Church became enriched with new definitions, new problems also, ever opening and insoluble, increased in number, and, within the limits thus laid down, reason, history, and common sense endeavoured to maintain their rights in such a manner as to threaten, at every moment, to break through the still recent enclosure of ecclesiastical dogma. Apollinaris had touched the true difficulty. The more entire was the deity of Jesus, so much the more imperiously did the question of his humanity press upon the minds of theologians. They had maintained against Apollinaris the complete human nature of Jesus; but they had been obliged to distinguish so carefully the divine from the human nature in him, that they had come in this way to separate them, and to speak as if the divine Word had taken to itself (συνῆψεν ἑαυτῷ) a perfect man; the two natures being thus conjoined, but not united in his single personality. Diodorus of Tarsus and Theodorus of Mopsuesta, both pupils of the school of Antioch, and many others with them, strongly maintained that view. One step more in this direction, and the return would have been made purely and simply to the old Unitarianism, to the man Jesus, acted upon and inspired by the Spirit, or the divine Word. In vain, truly, would it have proved that Arianism had been trampled down at Nicæa and Constantinople!

Nestorius was the bishop of Constantinople from the year 428. He had to contend with jealous rivalries, and against his fellow-bishop Cyril of Alexandria, who persecuted the memory of Chrysostom, even in the person of a successor who desired to do it justice. Nestorius sympathized with those who separated the two natures, from fear of annihilating the divine nature by lowering it, or the human nature by taking from it one or other of its constituent elements. In particular, he refused to call Mary *Mother of God* (Θεοτόκος), on the ground, as he said, that God has no mother, that the Creator cannot be born of a creature, and that Mary could only have given birth to the human nature which the divine

Word willed to make its organ. Cyril did all within human power to stir up the minds of the people against Nestorius. He had the address to prejudice against him Celestinus, bishop of Rome, by leading him to believe that Nestorius favoured the Pelagians, who were looked upon at the time with great disfavour in the West. Both at Rome and at Alexandria, Nestorius was convicted of heresy; and the dispute grew more and more bitter, till Theodosius II. thought it necessary to convoke an Œcumenical Council at Ephesus in 431. On this, as on former occasions, the affirmative party overruled the negative. The person of Mary began to rise in the new empyrean. The paradoxical name of *Mother of God* pleased the popular piety. Nestorius was condemned, and died in exile in 440. The Council decided that Christ was at the same time God and man (Θεὸς ὁμοῦ καὶ ἄνθρωπος), and that in the unity of his person the two substances, the divine and human, were not simply annexed, but united. Yet it was not explicit as to the mode of this union, still less as to its possibility. The Council thus affirmed the contradiction that Nestorius and those who thought with him sought to avoid, but it did nothing to solve it. Nestorianism, though it was proscribed throughout the Roman empire, succeeded in maintaining its ground in the Persian empire. The school of Edessa was its chief centre, the policy of the Persian kings leading them to encourage a division which broke the tie between their Christian subjects and the imperial Church. The Nestorian Church, which extended its branches as far as China, has continued in the East even to our own days.

The Council of Ephesus, in decreeing the dogma of the two natures, still left the door open to views closely akin to Nestorianism. For example, it appeared to authorize those explications of certain difficult passages in the evangelical history which affirmed that Jesus, as a man, was ignorant of, or said what, as God, he knew or would not have said. This was in fact to separate his person into two consciousnesses and two wills—in other words, into two persons. At Alexandria, Cyril and his successor Dioscurus opposed with the greatest energy this doctrine of the two natures, whilst Eutychus, who maintained it, was condemned at Constantinople. Then it was, in 449, that the Council was held which was called the Robber Synod of Ephesus, a general Council in which Dioscurus forced the bishops to decide in his favour. But protestations poured in from all sides; and the death of Theodosius II., by raising to the throne Marcian and Pulcheria, furnished to the advocates of the two natures an opportunity for a signal retaliation. The bishop of Rome, Leo I., had pronounced formally against Eutychus; the Council of Chalcedon, the fourth Œcumenical Council, condemned Dioscurus, and all who along with him rejected the dogma of the two natures. It was understood, therefore, that Jesus was true man and true God, uniting in himself the two natures "without confusion, without change, without division, without separation, each of the two natures preserving its own proper characteristics," but the unity of his person remaining unaltered. Let any one understand this who can, if indeed it ever has been understood! Although it was invested with imperial sanction, although the partisans of Dioscurus were henceforth branded as *Monophysite* heretics, Palestine and Egypt rose against the decree of Chalcedon, and still continued to adhere to the condemned Monophysism.

Monophysism consisted, not in denying that the Son had participated in humanity, but in reducing his human nature to unconscious, impersonal elements; so that the consciousness, the will, in a word the personality of Jesus, was unique, and that of a God. This was a revival in another form of the doctrine of Apollinaris. It was, besides, the logical continuation of the idea of Athanasius, but this also in its turn now gave umbrage to the Christian feeling, which preferred to resign itself to an intellectual contradiction rather than not to see in Jesus a true man making but one with a true God.

We will spare our readers the recital of the dreary and subtile disputes which were continued long after the Council of Chalcedon. For example, the Emperor Zeno the Isaurian, in 482, hoped to make peace by drawing up a *Henotikon;* but this, although it was agreed to by the bishop of Alexandria of the time, still more increased the confusion, since the Roman bishops were strongly in favour of the strict maintenance of the doctrine of Chalcedon, whilst the *Henotikon* made some concessions to the Monophysites. Justinian, who ascended the throne in 527, also tried to re-establish concord, but was not more successful in his efforts. Monophysism, entrenching itself in Egypt, as in an impregnable fortress, became more completely separated from the rest of Christendom. The Arabian conquest rendered this schism irrevocable, and thus was constituted what is now called the *Coptic Church*. The Christians of Armenia, who had adopted the *Henotikon* of Zeno, formally declared themselves Monophysites in 595. It is under this form that they have preserved their organization and their ecclesiastical autonomy until the present day. The scattered fragments of the Monophysites in Syria and Mesopotamia re-organized under the direction of Jacob Baradaï (541—578), formed themselves into societies named after him the Jacobite communities.

But this was not all. The Emperor Heraclius (611—641) was also possessed with the desire to bring the Monophysites back to the Church, and he thought that if it were conceded to them that there was only one "active will" in the person of Christ, they might without much difficulty conform to the Catholic dogma. This originated, however, one more heresy, called *Monothelism*. How could it be admitted, if there were in

Jesus both a true man and a true God, that either the man or the God was deprived of personal will? On the other hand, were not the Monophysites in some measure right in alleging that two wills necessarily implied two persons? After many debates, a sixth Œcumenical Council had to be held at Constantinople in the year 680, under Constantine Pogonatus, when it was decided that Jesus, as God-man, possessed two wills, the one divine, the other human, but that the latter was always and invariably in submission to the all-powerful divine will; which was in fact to deny what was at the same time affirmed. The same method was always followed, inspired by the same interest, rather religious than logical, indicating the insuperable difficulty in which the Church found itself. Monothelism, which flourished for a short time at Constantinople under Philippicus Bardanes (711—713), was perpetuated amongst the Maronites* of the Lebanon until the time of the Crusades.

The East had had the monopoly of these disputes in which the Greek Church was exhausting itself. Who can say to what degree this exhaustion, along with the grave objections which the ecclesiastical doctrine of the Trinity raised, favoured the rapid conquests of Mussulman Monotheism? Western Christendom came more promptly to a conclusion upon these questions, which

---

* So named from John Maro, their first independent patriarch, who died in 701.

were as much metaphysical as religious; and taking them on their mystic rather than their speculative side, it succeeded in framing definitively the formula of that immense movement of ideas which had been worked out for the most part in the East. The eminent theologians of the West had always supported, or accepted, the orthodoxy enunciated in the East. The most illustrious of them, Augustine, whose not very original genius would never have conceived the bold speculations in which the oriental mind delighted, accepting the Catholic tradition blindly and without question, excelled in the art of presenting in a clear and methodical form; and with a power due to his own rich imagination and his sympathetic mysticism, the still ill-arranged ideas of the orthodox system; and it is to him that the dogma of the Trinity really owes its completion.

This tendency of his mind led him in fact to seek for the means of rendering the Trinitarian dogma, if not conceivable by human reason, at least endurable by it. He hoped to succeed in rounding, so to speak, the acute angles of the orthodox doctrine. For instance, he tried to efface the last vestiges of the ancient subordination, either by showing that it was not necessary to give a human sense to the expressions *Sent, Generation* of the Son, and *Procession* of the Holy Spirit, or by maintaining that in every divine act the whole Trinity co-operated.*

* It was in this way that he combated the old view, so dear to Tertullian and the first advocates of the Word, according to which the theophanies

Upon the whole, he succeeded much better in bringing the three terms to unity than in keeping each one distinct. More than once he acknowledged that this doctrine was one of which it must be said, *pie credendum est*, and that the "natural man" cannot comprehend it.[*] The analogies drawn from human nature, which he developed with the greatest evident satisfaction, amply confirm this view of his teaching. "Thus," he said, "when we mentally represent to ourselves an outward object, we distinguish between the memory of that object, the inner vision of it, and the will which brings these together. Here are three distinct elements, the unity of which forms one thought."[†] So, again, finding in the human mind a faint image of the Creator, he perceives a sort of trinity in its memory of itself, its self-consciousness, and self-love, qualities quite distinct, and yet united in the indivisible unity of the human person. The comparison, though ingenious, and of undoubted philosophical value, is nevertheless an unfortunate one, and it does not succeed in making the Trinity intelligible. For the point is to show how these three distinct divine persons do not make three Gods, and not, what is never disputed, that distinct faculties may belong to a single person. Like all theorists on the Trinity,

and divine interventions of the Old Testament were imputed, not to the Father, but to the Son. This view necessarily implied the inferiority of the Son; and Augustine sagaciously perceived that, if the least concession were made on this point, Arianism and what would be still worse might follow.

[*] *De Trinit.* vii. 2.   [†] *Ibid.* xi. 6.

Augustine, in order to avoid the Charybdis of Tritheism, is in peril of striking upon the Scylla of Sabellianism. The rigid conditions of the notion of personality counteract all his efforts, and indeed he does not conceal from himself the inadequacy of any such analogy. But then of what use was it?

Augustine was no happier in his efforts to render the dogma of the two natures acceptable. His favourite idea was that Jesus Christ was man and God in one single person, just as each one of us is flesh and spirit.* If this analogy were to be taken in its strict sense, would it not lead directly to the condemned doctrine of Apollinaris, and consequently to Monophysism?

But, we must not cease to repeat, these errors in sound logic were not even noticed at the time. Western Christendom had not the slightest intention of repudiating the metaphysical decrees of the East. The controversy on Pelagianism moved it much more deeply than that on the deity of Jesus. Augustine rivetted a dogma already firmly fixed in the Latin Church. For a moment only the West had taken the opposite side of the great Eastern controversies. The Councils of Spain, in order to remove the venom of Arianism, had often made use of this formula, that the Son was such *naturâ, non adoptione*, meaning that the Son owed his being to an internal necessary determination of the divine substance, and not to the adventitious willing of the Father. But

* *Enchir.* 36.

Victorinus, Isidore of Seville, and several other Spanish theologians, starting from this point, taught that the man Jesus was, on the contrary, Son of God *by adoption*. In the eighth century, this idea, which was really only a half-disguised Nestorianism, received the favour of Elipand, archbishop of Toledo, and of Felix, bishop of Urgel. Their opinions, which were highly appreciated in Spain, penetrated into France, and drew the attention of Charlemagne, who desired nothing better than to follow in the steps of the Roman Emperors in everything. At Frankfort and Aix-la-Chapelle (794 and 799), *Adoptionism*, strenuously opposed by Alcuin, was condemned in the persons of its representatives. Elipand, protected by his Moorish king, refused to retract. Felix was more docile; but it is evident from documents belonging to him which were found after his death that his submission had been forced. With the decease of the two Adoptionist chiefs, the doctrine declined. It could strike no deep roots in an age even more unfavourable than the third or fourth centuries were to rationalistic tendencies. Nevertheless, from time to time the history of the Church has to record the appearance of an occasional Adoptionist, or at least of a defender of Adoptionism, such as, for example, the Jesuit Vasquez and the Protestant Professor Calixtus.*

---

* Comp. for the history of Adoptionism, Gieseler, *Kirchengesch.* ii. i. § 13; Baur, *Dreieinigkeit*, ii. i. ch. iv.; the article *Adoptionismus* in the *Encyclopédie* of Herzog.

About the same time we find in common use in the West a confession of Trinitarian faith of uncertain origin, probably composed in Spain, but of which we have no authentic record prior to the eighth century. It has been attributed, without reason, to Augustine; but to call it the *Creed of Athanasius* is to bid defiance to history. Originally written in Latin, as is proved by the many various readings of the Greek text, this Creed, frequently called also the Symbol *Quicumque*, from the word with which it begins, is properly an extension of the Creeds of Nicæa, Constantinople, Ephesus, and Chalcedon. It is so composed as to define the Trinitarian dogma in all its paradoxical severity, while closing up every fissure that might still allow passage to any breath of heresy to enter in, and threatening all who deny it with everlasting condemnation. This Creed, then, sums up the results of Christian thought during the first seven centuries, and the veneration with which it came to be regarded in the Church as corrupted by orthodoxy proves how completely it answered to the tendencies of the age. It was soon held, as in some churches it is still considered to be, one of the most sacred documents of Christianity. Its popularity was not in the least affected by the simple audacity, or, as we may venture to call it, the gross plainness of speech, with which the contradictions of the orthodox theology are enumerated, and so precisely stated that one might almost believe at times that it was an opponent exaggerating in order that he might the better refute them. This was far, however, from being the case. Christian piety had long delighted in contradictions. In this Creed will be seen the topstone placed on the edifice so laboriously erected in honour of the deity of Christ.

"*Quicumque vult servari,*" it says; "whosoever will be saved, before all things it is necessary that he hold the Catholic faith, which every one must keep whole and undefiled, if he will not to perish everlastingly. And the Catholic faith is this, that we worship one God in Trinity, and Trinity in Unity; neither confounding the Persons nor dividing the Substance.

"For there is one Person of the Father, another of the Son, and another of the Holy Spirit. But the Godhead of the Father, of the Son, and of the Holy Spirit, is one, their glory equal, their majesty co-eternal. Such as the Father is, such is the Son, and such is the Holy Spirit. The Father is uncreated, the Son uncreated, and the Holy Spirit uncreated; the Father is incomprehensible, the Son incomprehensible, and the Holy Spirit incomprehensible; the Father eternal, the Son eternal, the Holy Spirit eternal.

"And yet they are not three eternals, but one eternal; as also there are not three incomprehensibles, nor three uncreated, but one uncreated, and one incomprehensible. So likewise the Father is Almighty, the Son is Almighty, and the Holy Spirit Almighty. And yet they are not three Almighties, but one Almighty. So the Father is

God, the **Son** is God, and the Holy Spirit is God. And yet they are not three Gods, but one God. So likewise the Father is Lord, the Son is Lord, and the Holy Spirit Lord; and yet they are not three Lords, but one Lord. **For** like as we are compelled by the Christian verity to acknowledge each Person by himself (*singillatim*) **to be** God and Lord, so are we forbidden by the Catholic religion to say that there are three Gods and three Lords.

"The Father is neither made, nor created, nor begotten. The Son is of the Father alone, neither made, nor created, **but begotten. The** Holy Spirit is of the Father and of the Son, neither made, nor created, nor begotten, but proceeding. So there is but one Father, not three Fathers; one Son, not three Sons; one Holy Spirit, not three **Holy** Spirits. And in this Trinity none is afore or after another; none is greater or less than another; but the three Persons are together co-eternal and equal. So that in all things, as is afore said, the Unity in Trinity, and the Trinity in Unity, is to be worshipped. He, therefore, that will be saved must thus think of **the Trinity.**

"Furthermore, it is necessary to everlasting salvation that he also believe rightly concerning the incarnation of our Lord Jesus Christ. Now the right faith is, that we believe and confess that our Lord Jesus Christ, the Son of God, is God and man; God of the substance of the Father, begotten before the ages, and man of the substance of his mother, born in time; perfect God and perfect man, possessing a reasonable soul and human flesh; equal to the Father as touching his Godhead, and inferior to the Father as touching his manhood. Who, although he be God and man, yet he is not two, but one Christ; one, not by conversion of the Godhead into flesh, but by taking of the manhood into God; one, in sum, not by confusion of substances, but by unity of person. For as the reasonable soul and flesh make one man, so God and man make one Christ:

"Who suffered for our salvation, descended into hell, was raised again the third day from the dead. He ascended into heaven; he sitteth on the right hand of the Father, God Almighty; from whence he shall come to judge the living and the dead. At whose coming all men shall rise again with their bodies, and must give account of their works. And they that have done good shall go into eternal life, and they that have done evil into eternal fire.

"This is the Catholic faith, which except a man believe faithfully and firmly, he cannot be saved."

Does any one desire to form an idea of the distance which separates the original and authentic Christianity from this orthodox Christianity fabricated by the Councils? Let him, after reading this cento of contradictions imposed upon faith under pain of hell, open the New Testament and read once more the Sermon on the Mount!

SECOND PERIOD.

ABSOLUTE DOMINATION OF THE DOGMA,

FROM THE COMMENCEMENT OF THE MIDDLE AGES TO THE EVE OF THE REFORMATION.

CHAPTER VII.

CATHOLIC ORTHODOXY.

The Christian sentiment had now attained the supreme object of its age-long aspirations. The Son of Man of the three first Gospels, having first become "the man from heaven," had then been identified with God the Word, and afterwards being more and more equalled with the Father in essence, eternity, power, and dignity, had completed his glorious ascension, without, however, being separated from his human nature, which was associated with all the steps of his apotheosis. The absolute deity of Christ, true man and true God, was henceforth taught by all the Christian authorities as an immutable, most sacred verity; and the pains of an eternal hell, as well as those of earthly justice, threatened the bold man who should venture to deviate, on even a single point, from the doctrine decreed by the Councils, and sanctioned by the bishops of Rome. In the matter of orthodoxy, the whole period of the middle ages had to live upon the capital amassed by the previous centuries at the cost of so many struggles. This repose of Christian thought lasted for eight hundred years.

In order to criticise fairly a dogma like this, it is not sufficient either to demonstrate its contingent character by showing how it originated, or to exhibit its illogical nature by bringing it to the tribunal of reason. This would not account for the power it exercised over the human soul for centuries, and especially for its influence over minds to which it would be impossible to attribute defect either in intellectual vigour or in the love of truth. The dogmas of the Trinity and the Incarnation are terrible burdens for us of modern times. Their essence is contradiction, that negation of the understanding; and our education has rendered us incapable of that docility in presence of the absurd which constituted, in former times, the distinguishing virtue of the religious man. And yet, even in our days, it is not uncommon to meet with serious men who have closed their ears against the dictates of common sense, whilst yielding to the still powerful charm of the dogmatic mysticism of Athanasius and Augustine, and who have even arrived at the point of utter bewilderment at our opposition, which they charge with pride and vain obstinacy. How must it have been, then, at the time when the strongest minds found no difficulty in accepting ecclesiastical dogmas in both **form** and substance, and the Trinity shone in the heavens of faith more manifest, more radiant than the noon-day summer's sun!

If religious psychology were more studied, we should understand better the deep-lying causes of the triumph and the decay of dogmas. It would be particularly interesting to know how far, and from what cause, the human mind endures for centuries an evident contradic**tion, and yet** becomes at last ashamed **of** this self-abdication—nay, absolutely incapable of so committing what appears to it henceforth as a mere act of suicide.

The dogma of the Trinity proclaimed its contradictions with an unflinching bravery. The Deity divided into three persons, *and yet* these three Divine persons forming only one God; of these three persons one only being self-existent, **the** two others deriving their existence from the first, *and yet* these three persons having to be considered as equal; each possessing his special **and** distinct character, the property peculiar to himself which is wanting in the other two, *and yet* all three being supposed each to possess the fulness of perfection —this was, it must be confessed, the deification of the contradictory. The dogma of the Incarnation, which taught the existence of a unique person composed of two natures, both personal, **and in** contradiction with each other at almost every point of their mutual contact, was not less irritating to the awakened reason; and this even the more because, notwithstanding all the efforts of the Fathers, the human nature of Christ, while preserved verbally in the creed, was not the less lost in the divine. It was God, after all, who was made man, and not the converse: the human consciousness was in fact absorbed in the divine consciousness; the human will was by necessity subject to the divine will. *And yet* orthodoxy still maintained that in the unique personality of Jesus there was a real man united to a real God. It became at last a mere contention of words.

To what, then, must we attribute the long and absolute domination of these two dogmas?

Is the authority of tradition, and faith in the infallibility of the teaching Church, a sufficient explanation? It is very true that, particularly in religion, tradition is a great power. In ordinary times almost all persons are prejudiced in favour of the beliefs of the past: they seem to those who are ignorant of history as though they must have always existed. Religious feeling naturally allies itself with the sense of weakness and with humility. The weight of the mysterious realities whose presence man feels, but which he cannot comprehend, inclines him to the side to which he thinks he can apply the really inapplicable rule, *Quod semper, ubique, ab omnibus creditum est*. The proof of this is, that where the charm of the tradition is broken, faith in this infallibility disappears.

All this is matter of experience; but experience shows also that, if tradition protects doctrines by diffusing over them a certain fragrance as of some emanation from the eternal spheres, the doctrines in their turn cause the tradition insensibly to lose its fascination, until at length it is no longer able to support them. This period arrives when the inconsistency of the dogma is so powerfully felt as to neutralize the attraction which it once possessed for the mind. So *powerfully* felt, we say; for it is not enough, as history also shows, that the contradictions of a religious doctrine should be perceived, to make that doctrine immediately lose its dominion. So long as the doctrine retains its charm for his heart, the believer finds some means of silencing or deluding his reason. Either he will establish a theory that faith and knowledge are properly distinct from each other, or, as more often happens, he will smooth the harsh points of the contradiction by compressing them, as it were, within the network of some conciliatory scheme more or less ingenious and arbitrary. He would not be the dupe of these half voluntary illusions if his reason were not led astray by his heart. In order, therefore, to explain the long subsistence of contradictory dogmas, as well as to give an account of their origin, we must discern in what aspects they have satisfied the religious sentiment. Dogmas in order to be believed must be loved.

We observe, in the first place, that, at a certain point

in the development of the human mind, the religious sentiment easily bears with what is contradictory in order of logic. It may even find real pleasure in so doing, although this is certainly not a sign of sound health. It is hypertrophy, and not health, when one organ is developed to such a degree as to enfeeble the others. But the fact is unquestionable. The religious man quickly learns to veil his face before the Infinite that he adores, and to acknowledge that he comprehends nothing of it. The contradictory soon becomes for him the paradoxical (and for that reason the more welcome), equivalent of the incomprehensible. It is a kind of sacrifice of his reason, an intellectual renunciation, bearing the semblance of a homage rendered to the indefinable Power whose immensity confounds his thought. Is it not, in these days, the perpetual strain of minds that have not outgrown the feelings and traditions of the middle ages—this incessant appeal to the unfathomable mystery? As though the mysterious and the contradictory were identical!

In the second place, it should be acknowledged that both the dogmas in question appealed eloquently to the religious sense. That of the Incarnation, at least in its intention, brought God near to man, and man near to God in such a manner as to sanctify human nature, without apparently lowering the Divine Majesty. As to the dogma of the Trinity, its religious eloquence, though less immediate in effect, was not less real. The

Trinitarian God is a living God. He is not the unknown principle seated at the centre of all things, blind and deaf, producing worlds like a fermenting substance without knowing either what He is or what He does. Nor, again, is He the purely ideal term of the "Universal Becoming," *that* God in process of continual evolution, who does not create the world, but is created by the world; a *future* God who will be, but at present is not, or who at least only murmurs as yet in the cradle of the human consciousness. Finally, He is not the dreary God of Deism, that supreme mechanician retired within the icy depths of his own eternity, and without permanent and active connection with the work of his capricious genius. Neither of these Gods is a being we can worship. To present them to the human spirit hungering after religion, is like giving stones to the poor instead of bread. The idea of the indwelling of God in the world has done more to banish the Trinity from religious minds than all the arguments of criticism. With this view men have felt themselves once more in the presence of a real God, one near at hand; and the soul has been moved, as of old, at the touch of his spirit. But in the inveterate dualism which was at the foundation of the thought of the middle ages, and which we find in all the religious ideas of that time, such a conception would have found no point of support. The only true God must needs be a living God, and in that respect the triplicity of Divine persons satisfied the soul. The "infinite" was filled with the ineffable converse of the Father with the Son, of the Son with the Father, to whom the Holy Spirit responded with its eternal "Amen." And then, one of these persons became incarnate for us guilty men, to rescue us from the power of that great Devil in whom people believed at least as firmly as in God, and to make expiation by his sufferings for our innumerable sins. This God the Redeemer was not however the Father, who, as the official dogma itself declared, still remained in a sense the absolute—God in the full meaning of the word. Thus the contradictions of the dogma had the advantage of responding to two demands of the religious consciousness, which desired a God-man, but also a perfect God. If it were possible to forget what one knows, if the religious sentiment enlightened by science could still be satisfied with the irrational, the God of the Trinity might still be the God of our worship!

We must also remark that the Trinitarian dogma, made complete as it was at the commencement of the middle ages, seems as if it had been expressly framed for that period, a period of ignorance, but also of vigorous germination. It is in perfect harmony with everything besides which characterized the times of its unquestioned dominion. The middle ages were a kneading together of contradictions, social, political, and ecclesiastical, which, striving to become organized, and only partially succeeding, arranged themselves to the best of their power.

There was no unity, far from it; **yet the** desire for unity subsisted. Read once more the creed *Quicumque*, and see if the dogma which is set forth in its sharply-cut formulas, its subtilties, and its grand outlines, does not bear some resemblance to a Gothic cathedral. It shows the same daring, the same disregard of difficulties, **and the** same simplicity of means in warding off dangers that are too evident; something perplexed and forced, **but** yet ingenious; details odd and without symmetry; arches placed **on one** another contrary to all common **sense**; angles, points, and turrets, which jut out on all sides; the triple nave converging towards the single spire; hell in gloom beneath in the crypt, and paradise shining above through the openings of the vaulted roof; while yonder, in the holy of holies, the Son is taking flesh to save mankind.

We should notice, finally, one very important element in this explanation. Perhaps, notwithstanding all these causes so favourable to its prolonged sway, the dogma **of** the Trinity would have sooner met with opposition, had the general body of Christendom made the three Divine persons the exclusive, or even the main object **of their** devotion. Such was **by no** means the case. Strange and yet certain is it that this dogma was protected by what we may justly designate, looking at it from the Christian point of view, one of its most serious defects. Springing originally from the desire to exalt the person of Jesus, it had overreached its mark in this respect, that, as we have already said, the God had eclipsed the man. Now, the God-Jesus no longer sufficiently satisfied that need of mediation between us and God which man urgently feels at a certain stage of his spiritual development. But, in proportion as the Son of Man had been raised towards absolute deity, other beings had come in to fill the place which he left void. Veneration for angels, for saints, for the Virgin Mary, had increased in the Church in proportion to the deification of its Founder. It is this chiefly which has sustained the edifice of the Trinity amongst Catholic nations. The Trinitarian dogma soon lost its stability in the communities which grew out of the Reformation of the sixteenth century, all of which agreed in rejecting the adoration of created beings that had been encouraged in the ancient Church. But in the middle ages the absolute deity of Jesus was supported by all these relative divinities, forming a regular and graduated hierarchy. Mary especially, transfigured by the beams cast upon her by her Son, came to be looked upon more and more as a Christ-substitute, a lovely moon with light borrowed, but of an exquisite sweetness; and that painter who represented her as interposing between the Son and the world in order to turn aside the arrows of Christ's vengeance, though he doubtless fell into an enormous heresy according to the evangelical view, expressed the real sentiment of the Catholicism of the middle ages, and even that of our own day. What remained to complete the work was accomplished by the miraculous powers supposed to be conferred upon the clergy for the salvation of souls. The West, faithful to its characteristic tendency which dated back from the first centuries, was much more occupied with the means of salvation than with the person of the Saviour. The heresies, the monastic orders, the system of indulgences, achieved their popularity within this range of ideas, not in that of speculative questions. As to the East, which might have been animated by a very different spirit, the poor Greek Church, split up by its heresies, enervated by its emperors, and increasingly, though slowly crushed by the Moslem invasion, was but the shadow of its former self. The only Greek theologian who can be spoken of with honour during this period, except the learned Photius, is the monk John of Damascus, or the Damascene, in the eighth century, the editor of a species of orthodox *compendium* which was an authority in his Church for a thousand years, but which did not enrich the system with one original idea. He was merely the registrar of Greek orthodoxy.

Thus everything concurred to consolidate the rule of the Trinitarian dogma,—the authority of a tradition which derived its force from the universal ignorance; the aspects of it which, notwithstanding its crying inconsistencies, responded to the aspirations of the religious mind; its close accordance with the general spirit of the age; and the aid which it received from certain new beliefs which arose as it became complete, in order to make up for one of its great defects. So strongly indeed did it seem established, that it could even be for some time believed that the great revolution of the sixteenth century would leave it untouched.

Our history, therefore, comes to a pause; but it would be still incomplete if we did not indicate the various currents of thought which were visible within the unity, always more apparent than real, of the Catholic faith. Very nearly, at times, notwithstanding the orthodoxy of men's intentions, was heresy on the point of shooting up from the depths to the surface.

This was the case with several of the Scholastic writers. The formula which sums up this massive philosophy is well known: *Per fidem ad intellectum*. Believe first, then try to understand. Though in principle docile, Scholasticism was revolutionary in spite of itself, simply because it set men thinking. The dogma of the Trinity, through its transcendent nature and its flagrant contradictions, naturally called forth the efforts of a faith that sought to justify itself to the reason. Thus we observe two very different conceptions formed of the Trinity, accordingly as the thinkers of the middle ages were Nominalistic or Realistic.

Nominalism denied the reality of general ideas. It saw in them only names, words, *flatus vocis*, without any real corresponding object (*universalia post res*); while Realism regarded them as the very substance of things, preceding and determining them absolutely (*universalia ante res*). By applying, then, to the Trinity the Nominalist conception, complete Tritheism was at once arrived at. According to Roscelinus, the founder of Nominalism, the Father, the Son, and the Holy Spirit, are three real persons, whose unity resides solely in the general idea of Deity. They have in common the Divine nature, as three angels or three men have in common the general idea of the angelic nature or the human nature. But this general idea has no real existence. There is nothing real in the Trinity but the three persons; their unity is a mere **word**. The Council of Soissons **of** 1093 condemned Roscelinus, but **it could not** suppress the Nominalist view with its inevitable consequences.

In the same way Realism must necessarily end in Sabellianism, that is to say, in the suppression of the Divine persons to the advantage of the substantial unity. Observe for example how Anselm of Canterbury, the father of the Realistic Scholasticism, understood the Trinity. Following Augustine, he sought his point of comparison in the human mind. The mind, said he, in thinking of itself, presents to itself an image which is like it, which differs from it as the object does from the **subject, but** which nevertheless can only be separated from it by an abstraction of the reason. Here is the distinction between the Father and the Son.* The Spirit in its turn represents the reciprocal love of

* *Monol.* 33.

the Father and the Son, who are both pure spirit, and love each other as such.* But who could fail to see what complete shipwreck is thus made of the personality of the Father, the Son, and the Holy Spirit in this conception of the Trinity?

We do not undertake to solve the question as to how Anselm, holding such views, managed to reconcile his Trinitarian theory with his celebrated doctrine of Redemption, which was based (1) upon the necessity of making to the infinitely outraged honour of the Father such a satisfaction as would permit His love to pardon His guilty creatures; and (2) upon the incarnation of the Son, who became man in order to offer to the Father in his sufferings the sufficient equivalent that he alone could provide;—which was the doctrine developed in the *Cur Deus Homo*. It is clear that, in this view of the incarnation, the Son must be conceived of quite otherwise than as merely the subjective thought of the Father. Evidently the security inspired by his orthodox intentions deceived the theologian as to the real nature of his theodicy. We should notice here, however, in the heart of the middle ages, a remarkable modification in the direction of Christian thought. The deity of Jesus Christ is no longer simply the expression of his personal greatness. Henceforth theology connects it much more closely than in former times with his human work. The *human* point of view recovers therefore something of its

* *Monol.* § 7.

rightful place. It is still only a germ, but a germ that will grow. The Fathers of Chalcedon did not foresee that, by their persistence in affirming against the Monophysites the complete reality of the human nature of Christ, they were preserving in the very heart of the Trinitarian dogma the element that would at a future time destroy it.

The solution of the real question was not however as yet advanced by this means a single step. The impossible could no more be accomplished in the middle ages than in our own times; and even when the attempt was made to rise above the absolute mutual opposition of Realism and Nominalism, so soon as thought was directed to the Trinity it was forced to become heterodox. To take the example of Abelard, who owes his high reputation to his Conceptualism. According to this view, general ideas exist in God and in the human mind as necessary forms of thought. Hence it follows that what is general in God is also real. "Now God," says Abelard, "is absolutely perfect, *summa boni perfectio;* and absolute perfection resolves itself into *power, wisdom, and goodness.*" Here are the Father, the Son, and the Holy Spirit, the three *names,* as he does not shrink from designating them in the same passage,*— three names which together represent the absolutely one and indivisible substance, *uniquam et singularem, individuam penitus ac simplicem substantiam.* Where,

* *Theol. Christ.* i. 1.

then, does Abelard find the Trinity of persons? It is true that he is not always himself faithful to this conception. He compares the Trinity elsewhere to the three persons of the verb, the one speaking, the one spoken to, and the one that is spoken of. But then in what does the unity consist, save in that impersonal nature which is common to the three persons, a doctrine surely of distinct Tritheism!

Gilbert de Poitiers in his turn, although a Realist, falls into *Quatrideism*. "Divinity," he says, "is not God, any more than humanity is a man. We must not say, God is Father, Son, and Holy Spirit; for the Father, the Son, and the Holy Spirit are each respectively God, and they are one only by the divinity that is common to them." But this idea of an abstract divinity existing independently of the three persons, was not commonly accepted, and he was reproached with teaching the existence of four Gods. Peter the Lombard, at the end of his *Sentences and Distinctions*, found himself face to face with the same "tetracephalous monster," and Joachim of Flores bitterly reproached him with it. Joachim was condemned by the Lateran Council of 1215, which entirely approved of the definitions of the Lombard. Yet he it was who imagined the comparison which has been since admitted into orthodox symbolism, between the Trinity and the three angles of a triangle—a comparison which halts like all the others, since in order to make it hold good each angle should have all the properties of the triangle, and the triangle those of the angles.

Richard of St. Victor was the most ingenious of the Scholastics in his Trinitarian theory. "In God," says he, "is supreme goodness, and therefore perfect love. Now love must relate to another than oneself. The love of God then must have had an object eternal as God himself. No creatures, moreover, could be worthy of it. God needs therefore an uncreated being, another God. And then, each of the two divine persons desires a third person who shall be loved also as they love each other; for love between two, exclusive of every other object, is still but a species of egoism. This is the reason why the Trinity is composed of three persons divine, equal, and perfect." An explanation of this kind particularly pleased the mystics. Yet it was only, if closely considered, a hopeless resort, and it overlooked entirely the alternative which the modern philosophy would not have failed to suggest, that the living God needs either the Son or . . . the world. It assumed the personal existence of the Holy Spirit in a manner which bordered too closely on the absurd; or, if on this point also it must be taken seriously, why stop short on such a promising road? If love between two is still egoistical, is not love between three only a little less so? And might we not put in a claim for the existence of an infinitude of Gods loving each other with an infinite love? Besides, why should not creatures be *worthy* of eternal love?

Would it not be characteristic of an infinite love, that it should extend to those objects who are most unworthy of it? Lastly, if the theory be admitted, we see clearly the persons, we see the unity of essence and of love which binds them to each other; but where is the one God? We have thus three Gods who are one in heaven, as a father, his son, and his grandson may be one on earth. This is still Tritheistic.

Thomas Aquinas was more cautious. He taught that we may very well acquire by natural reason the knowledge of the unity of God, but not that of the distinction of the divine persons. "To undertake to prove the faith by arguments which are not conclusive," he said, "is to expose oneself to the mockery of the unbelieving. It is enough to show the possibility of what faith teaches."* He and Duns Scotus therefore sought in the human mind for analogies, not for proofs, but the abstruse subtilties in which their argumentation became involved did not contribute to clear up the question.†

In this rapid review of the theology of the middle ages, we must also mention some few thinkers who were attached to the traditional dogma less for its own sake than on account of the ideas or sentiments which took shelter under its consecrated formulas. For example,

* *Somme*, Part i. sec. 32, art. 1.
† See the critical exposition in detail of their theodicy in the second volume of the *History of the Dogma of the Trinity*, by F. C. Baur.

at the commencement of this period stands forth a giant of speculative thought, a figure strange and grave, isolated like a granite column in an open plain, looking back towards the Alexandrians through the medium of Dionysius the Areopagite whose theosophical reveries he translated, and at the same time suggesting already the idea of the Hegelian interpretation of the dogmas of the Church. We speak of the Irishman John Scot Erigena, to whom the world appeared as a theophany, the Son as the re-uniting of the finite with the infinite, and religion and philosophy as the double form of one and the same reality. It is he who comprises the totality of being in these four dialectic forms proceeding one from the other in order to return to the first:—that which is not created and which creates; that which creates and is created; that which is created and does not create; that which does not create and is not created. The first and the fourth form is the Father, the source and end of all things; the two others represent the Son, the principle of primordial causes, and the Holy Spirit, the principle of differences, of specializations, of the finite. This kind of dialectic may sound orthodox, but it is in reality far removed from the dogmas of the Church. Happily for himself, Erigena was not understood in his own time (the ninth century), and his idealistic Pantheism was not positively censured by the Church until the thirteenth century. Its condemnation was provoked by the extension of a mysticopantheistic school, of which Amalric of Béna and David of Dinant were the most noted representatives. In their system God was the essence, the origin, and the end of every creature. The incarnation was eternal. Every pious man was in a special manner an incarnation of the Holy Spirit, a Christ in whom God became man.

Some other mystics did not deviate so far from orthodoxy. But notwithstanding their endeavours to preserve fidelity to it, their mysticism at times got the better of their good intentions. In the twelfth century, Joachim of Flores, whom we have already named, being painfully moved by the corruption of the Church, attached to the dogma of the Trinity his reforming views set forth in apocalyptic language; and it was from his writings that the rigid Franciscans took the substance of their *Eternal Gospel*, which distinguished, after the manner of Sabellius, between the reign of the Father, that is of the law; that of the Son, that is of the New Testament; and that of the Holy Spirit which was about to come, and in which man in direct communion with God would be emancipated from all authority. An inevitable tinge of Pantheism always colours that order of speculations which makes out of the history of the world a history of God; and besides, an ardent mysticism, absorbed in the desire for union with the Eternal essence, is as much inclined as abstract thought to recognize no real distinction between the Creator and the creature. This was the case with the great German mystics of the later middle ages, Master Eckart, John Tauler, Ruysbroek, Henry Suso, and others. The dogma of the Incarnation was to them little more than the typical expression of the idea that the higher life of the spirit is a life of God within us, and the divine essence the abyss in which the regenerated soul is absorbed, passing from one delight to another in the ocean of blessedness. A God who is born, who suffers, who dies to live again, this was for them the crowning thought and the supreme joy.

But they had clearly no conception that they were introducing a heterogeneous element into the dogma that was in vogue. Nothing in their writings, any more than in those of the Scholastics, indicates as yet any change in the popular faith on the subject of the deity of Christ. Among the sects of the middle ages we scarcely find any but the Cathari who knowingly dissented from the ecclesiastical dogma. In their system, Satan and Christ were equally sons of God by their origin, understanding this in the Arian sense. Christ alone remained obedient; hence his struggle against the rebellious Satan, and his redemptive work for the salvation of men, whom Satan desired to keep in bondage. Neither the Waldenses nor the precursors of the Reformation, such as Huss, Wickliffe, and Wessel Gansfort of Groningen, although they treated with great boldness the dogmas of the Church, thought of carrying their heresies so far. One thing is evident, that they were wearied of Scholasticism and abstract reasonings. Like the moderate mystics of the same period, the author of the *Imitation of Christ* for example, they have no longer any confidence in school speculations, and prefer to limit themselves to the purely religious and practically edifying aspects of the Trinity and the Incarnation; a fact which proves that the absolute domination of these two dogmas is near its end. If men are still attached to them, it is no longer because of their truth, but for their usefulness. Though not able or bold enough to throw off the yoke, they try to turn it to the best possible advantage. When this point is reached in regard to dogmas their decline has obviously begun.

THIRD PERIOD.

CONTINUOUS DECLINE OF THE DOGMA,

FROM THE REFORMATION TO OUR OWN DAYS.

CHAPTER VIII.

PROTESTANT ORTHODOXY.

THE title of this chapter, viewed in relation to the general character that we assign to the third and last period of our history, will perhaps at first appear very paradoxical. It is generally thought that, if the Reformation was wonderfully bold in its manner of considering many very important points of the old traditions, it was eminently conservative, at least in the action of its most celebrated representatives, in all that concerns the doctrines of the Trinity and the Incarnation. Who does not at once recall to mind how sadly it belied itself by approving with almost entire unanimity of the burning of Servetus in honour of the Trinity? There are, however, historians who affirm that a closer examination will modify this first impression; and we are of their opinion. It is a very superficial judgment which estimates a new principle by only the first applications which are made of it. Ought we to identify the spirit of the Revolution of 1789 with that of the old government in France, because the Convention believed itself compelled to imitate the usages of despotism by organizing the Reign of Terror? No doubt the death of Servetus is a blot upon the history of Protestantism. But it remains to be considered whether, in the paroxysm of intolerance of which the unfortunate Spaniard was the victim, the historian is not justified in seeing at least an indication of the apprehensions which the first Protestants felt when they saw certain inevitable consequences arise from the very principle which they were so eager to proclaim with regard to the ancient Church.

We cannot mistake this principle when we endeavour to find the common characteristic of the manifestations of Protestant thought during and after the sixteenth century. It is that of the direct, personal communion of the believer with God, without any intermediate agent. This does not at all exclude the aids which an individual may find, and ought to seek, in the organized religious society, in the pastoral ministry, in the sacred books, and in common worship. But the relation is reversed. Whilst formerly it was the Church, in principle, which made the Christian, henceforth it is the Christians who will make the Church. The emancipation of the individual from all external spiritual authority is only the legitimate consequence of such an inversion. The *justification* of each man by *faith*, that is by an entirely personal, inward disposition, and no longer by sacraments, absolutions, and other outward means offered by the priesthood, became the formula of religious liberty. It was for this reason that the Reformation showed so bold a front in all that concerns the direct union of man with God. Just as it affirmed whatever strengthens this union and draws it closer, so was it the negation of everything that would lessen or suppress it. Of what use henceforth was that absurdity of transubstantiation, or those indulgences, those works of pious merit, the absolution of the priest, monastic vows, pilgrimages, relics, the intercessions of the saints, the mediation of Mary? Of what avail were all these, from the moment that the child of God knew that he was in direct, inalienable communion with the Omnipotent One of whose grace he partook? What signified to him the wretched dream of purgatory, and what could the Mass do for the salvation of his soul? If any one disputed his right thus to rise against the teaching of the infallible Church, his defence was ready. He had his Bible, which he now read without asking leave of any one; and though he read it as yet very imperfectly, he clearly saw enough to prove how complete was the dissimilarity between the Apostolic and the Romish Churches, and to teach him what to think of the infallibility and immutability claimed by the latter. It was in vain henceforth for the Vatican to brandish its keys and to declare that none could enter heaven without its permission. What insolence was this, to offer to the children of God the key of a mansion which already belonged to them, or, what was the same thing, belonged to God, their Father! Must permission be asked of an intruder to enter into one's own house?

The Reformation, then, was at once a great movement of piety and a grand assertion of liberty. We may even say that after it took place it would be very difficult, if not impossible, for liberty to be religious, and for piety to be free, without being more or less Protestant. But, besides that it is not in human nature to perceive at the first glance all the consequences of a principle, it would follow from the Reformation having so originated as it did, that the side on which the reformatory spirit first stormed the bastions of the old dogmatism would not be that of metaphysical dogma. Western Christendom remained faithful in the earlier period of this great contest to the practical tendency which, from the time of the first centuries, had always animated it. Questions of anthropological interest, such as those which concerned individual and social life, worship, and Christian morals, engaged much more of its attention than doctrines which had a less immediate application to the grand interests of salvation or of communion with God. It was no imperfectly solved question of the schools, it was the scandal caused by the sale of indulgences which set fire to the powder. Conscience had more to do with the movement of insurrection than learning, and therefore it was that it became so quickly popular.

The necessary result was that, being desirous of the triumph of its rightful claims, while forced to be circumspect by the atrocious means of repression directed against it, the Reformation was compelled by the instinct of self-preservation to appear as respectful as possible towards the traditional doctrines which did not directly touch the object it most dearly prized. It is so in all great revolutions. The number is always very considerable of those who are half-gained over to the principle, but recoil before its extreme consequences, which, moreover, the opponents of the principle never fail to portray in the most alarming colours. The adherents of it then try to prove clearly that they are not so black as they have been represented, and that there are still important points which are not in dispute. They are thus drawn on to exaggerate the conservative side of the new opinions, hoping by this means to facilitate the definitive establishment of that which they desire above all things to settle. The death of Servetus, and the intolerant measures from which the Antitrinitarians in general had to suffer amongst the Protestant nations, resulted entirely from this cause. Doubtless personal antipathy and the dictatorial disposition of Calvin contributed; but it must not be forgotten that these deplorable inconsistencies were either advised beforehand, or approved of afterwards, by the great majority of the first Protestants.*

* The more we study the lives of the Reformers of the sixteenth century, the more we are persuaded that their intolerance was the result of circumstances which appeared to them irresistible, and not the spontaneous fruit of their original conviction. For instance, in the first edition of his *Christian Institutes,* in 1536, Calvin said (p. 147) that "the excommunicated, as well as Turks, Saracens, and other enemies of religion, ought to be brought back to the unity of the Church only by persuasion, clemency, and prayer." We seek in vain for this passage in the later editions. This interesting remark is due to M. J. Bonnet (*Bulletin de la Société Historique du Protestantisme Français,* Nov. 1867). It is necessary, I think, to add an observation which is seldom made. When we say that conscience had more to do with the religious revolution of the sixteenth century than learning, it must be understood that we only mean that the former was predominant. The Renaissance and the Reformation were sisters. If knowledge had not been more diffused in the sixteenth century than in the middle ages, the movement would probably have been a failure, or at the best a mere local success. In fact, most of the Humanists sympathized with the Reformation. But when evil days came, when they would have been called upon to risk liberty and life, the scientific and literary element in great measure disappeared, especially in France and in the South. The men of energetic and immovable consciences remained almost alone. Hence the triumph of the doctrines which set forth the new principle in all its severity, and often even in the paradoxical form which gratifies religious passion. This explains also the popularity and influence of the Calvinistic dogma, which was in England, France, and Holland, the faith of men whom nothing could subdue. The defect of this heroism is, that it soon becomes bitter and hard. Calvin was a dictator, as the man who energetically represents the principle of resistance at any price always will be, in any community that is menaced with destruction. In such times men harden themselves against reverses and sufferings, but, while so little sparing themselves, they run a great risk of becoming hard towards others also. It is now proved that, if Calvin is responsible for the grievous wrong of desiring the death of Servetus, he made vain efforts to save him from the stake (J. Bonnet, l.c.; Rilliet, *Relation du Procès Criminel contre Michel Servet.* p. 122). This diminishes the odium attending his conduct, without excusing it. But, admitting all this, we need not be unjust to one of the founders of our language, one of the most

Still it was, after all, the Reformers and their most orthodox disciples who, without intending it, initiated the decline of the Trinitarian dogma. While they fully believed that they were preserving it, they introduced into it modifications which tended to its utter destruction. It was the new importance imparted by their principle itself to the essential relation between man and God, that urged them on in this direction, and to continue in it they had only to follow the connecting thought which was left in the old dogma, in its defence of the real humanity of Christ in conjunction with his absolute deity.

At first they did not greatly care to give any attention to the subject. Melancthon, in his *Loci Communes* of 1523, a first essay towards the systematizing of the new doctrine, did not even touch upon either the Trinity or the Incarnation. These dogmas appeared to him, as it would seem, outside the gospel. He foresaw with remarkable sagacity the "tragedies" which discussions on the Trinity would not fail to produce.* Luther at first spoke in much the same manner. Both changed their opinions later, and dogmatized upon the Trinity. But Lutheranism adopted a novel view of the subject, celebrated in the history of theology under the name of *Communication of Attributes*.

This view was less connected with new metaphysical profound thinkers of the French nation, and, lastly, to the man who stamped with the seal of his religious genius the only peoples that for a long period have been able to gain and to guard their liberties.

* Letters to Camerarius and Brenz in the year 1533.

speculations than with the need which was felt to give support to the Lutheran dogma respecting the Lord's Supper, a dogma which met the desire to bring man as near as possible to God. It is known that Luther, while rejecting transubstantiation, maintained the real, invisible presence of the body of Christ in the consecrated bread and wine. But he did not hold that a miracle contrary to nature was required as the condition of this real presence. How, then, could the body of Christ be present in so many places at the same time? In this way: the glorified body of Christ is omnipresent; like God himself, it possesses *ubiquity*. But how can a body possess ubiquity? This body is indivisibly united to the second person in the Trinity, and since the incarnation took place it is wherever that person itself is. Such was the basis of the theory of the *Communicatio Idiomatum* that was elaborated by the followers of Luther who himself only laid down its first premises, and which amounts to this, that the human nature of Jesus has become a participant in the proper attributes (*idiomata*) of the Deity. This theory was one likely to give birth to inextricable subtilties, and it did not fail to fulfil its promise. In truth, it did not take into account the earthly life of Jesus, when his human body was still subject to the limitations of place, and his human person was still far inferior to God. In order to overcome this difficulty, the hypothesis of *Occultation* was invented, according to which the incarnate Word hid for a time its divine glory, so as to appear a real man; which led directly to Docetism. Some persons preferred the hypothesis of *Exinanition*, in which view the Word, during its human life, became annihilated, by depriving itself of all that constituted its divinity; which leaves little assured as to the existence of God himself.

But we have not to discuss a doctrine of which no serious thinker could now even dream. We simply state what it was. It is evident that its source is to be found in the desire to establish an indissoluble metaphysical link between human nature in its totality and God. Luther and the old Lutherans meant absolutely that this human nature was become, through Christ, an integral part of the divine nature. It was no longer enough for them that God had entered into humanity; it was necessary besides that humanity, since the redemption, should have entered into the Deity. This doctrine found a strong point of support in the inclination of the German mind for whatever brings into unity the human nature and the divine. It entirely set aside the ancient doctrine of the two natures united in Jesus "without confusion, without change, each preserving its own properties."* There was this amount of truth in it, that it insisted upon the idea of an affinity, a natural relationship between God and man. It was connected in this respect with modern thought, and it augured a

---

* Definition of the Council of Chalcedon of 450.

deeper reformation. Man and the virtual greatness of his nature were henceforth made prominent. If human nature is so far capable of divine development, the dogma of the Incarnation is undermined, which would argue for the necessity of a descent of the Deity from the absolute incapability of human nature to raise itself towards God. Still further, the theory of *communicated attributes* suffered shipwreck by striking against the logical impossibility of attributing to material human nature properties entirely immaterial, and no subtilty could succeed in bringing it into accordance with the real Christ of the Gospel narrative.

The Calvinistic theology, while more sober in imagination, went further than Lutheranism in its involuntary remoulding of the old dogma. At first it appeared more attached to the Trinitarian tradition, and devoutly repeated the *Quicumque* Creed. And it must be allowed that it never officially detached itself from that tradition, though it did everything short of that. For example, one of its fixed axioms was, that the finite cannot contain the infinite, *infinitum non est capax infiniti*. It used this axiom against both the Catholic dogma of the Real Presence, and the Lutheran theory of the Communication of Attributes. If it applied it to the person of Jesus, while supposing itself faithful to the old dogmas, the result would be the following double assertion, which, if not somehow explained, would be a contradiction in terms: "The whole plenitude of the Deity dwelt in the human nature of Christ," and at the same time, "the whole Deity was without him." **How** could this be? In this way, that the Son, or the Word was not circumscribed or enclosed in the man Jesus; the Word while intimately united to him, never ceased to fill the infinite. In other words—and here we come to the actual result of the dogma of the Reformed Church—the Word was united to the man Jesus, so far as human nature, without being false to itself, was capable of embodying the divine perfection, *perfectio quæ in humanam naturam cadere possit.** If in the place of the Word we put here the Holy Spirit, which after all only differs from the Word in name, we are on the verge of the most decided Unitarianism.

What, in fact, are the divine attributes of which human nature is capable without ceasing to be itself? Are they omnipresence, omniscience, omnipotence? No, they are moral attributes,—holiness, justice, goodness. A man may possess all these and yet continue a man. The perfection of Jesus, therefore, is moral perfection, holiness, not absolute perfection. And accordingly Calvin distinguished himself above all the other expositors of past times by his serious acceptance of all those details of the evangelical history in which the truly human nature of Jesus is positively indicated.

---

* *Multa ineffabilia clara,* well said the *Admonitio* of the Reformers of the Palatinate (1581), *communicantur humanitati* **a Deitate**, *sed nulla ipsam* ***destruentia***. *Nulla natura in seipsâ recipit contradictoria.*

He did not shrink from recognizing in him a development, ignorance,* fatigue, sadness, nay, even moments of doubt.† Did Calvin himself see that his exegesis, which was very precise for his time, disposed of almost all the scriptural proofs generally brought forward in support of the Trinity? One thing is certain, that his Commentaries reduced them to nothing. According to him, even the very formula of baptism does not relate to the Trinity of the Divine Persons, but to the triple relation in which God stands towards man in the new economy. Gomar, J. de la Marck, and most of the fathers of Calvinism taught the same.

This positive sense of the humanity of Jesus asserted itself in other departments of the old "Reformed Church" theology. Thus the Church declared that, since the resurrection the man Jesus, always united to the Word, but always distinct from it as to his human person, occupies the first place amongst created beings; that he sheds upon us the divine grace; and that he is the living channel of that Spirit of God which gives us moral life, and infuses (*instillat*) into us the strength and the joy of heaven. Christianity then is essentially the communication of the divine life to man by the humanity of Jesus. With this parent idea is connected that intense Calvinistic mysticism, which, even with the bread and wine of the Supper before it, would not have attention fixed on these symbols, "as if the Lord

* *Comm. ad Luc.* ii. 40. † *Comm. ad Matt.* xxvii. 34.

were there enclosed in a gross and carnal manner," but which rather exhorted the communicant to soar in spirit into the heavenly regions, in order to purify his sinful humanity by uniting himself with the human substance of Jesus, who, on his part, shares his divine riches with those who nourish themselves from his personal life. In all this is shown the importance that was attached in the "Reformed" opinion to that humanity of Jesus which the earlier dogma verbally maintained, but really sacrificed to his deity.*

It was certainly in consequence of the same view that Calvin went so far as greatly to modify the strict notion of personality as applied to the three terms of the Trinity. The *persons*, according to him, become simply divine attributes, *discretæ in Deo proprietates*,† and most of his followers made no hesitation in defining them as modes, *existendi modi*. Evidently we are brought back to Sabellianism; if not to that of Sabellius himself, at least to the doctrine which the Fathers and the Councils condemned. In effect, the personality of Jesus, which in the old orthodoxy was a divine personality, becomes once more the human personality of the primitive Unitarianism. Mary can no longer be termed *Mother of God*. The orthodox Voetius goes so far as to

---

* Comp. the profound remarks upon the Calvinistic Christology in the works of Scholten, *De Leer der Hervormde Kerk* (in Dutch), Vol. ii. ch. vi. and viii.; Baur, *Gesch. der Dreieinigkeit*, Vol. iii.; Colani, *Revue de Théologie*, 1855, p. 349 and foll., &c.

† In John i. 1. Comp. *Institut.* i. xiii. 16.

count *faith* as one of the virtues of Jesus. But what especially characterizes the Calvinistic orthodoxy is, that, in declared opposition to Lutheran and Catholic usage, it denies that worship should be paid to Christ. This negation is logical if Christ or the Man-God possesses only a part of the Divine perfections. He may be, he is the Mediator, but he cannot be the object of that worship which can be properly addressed only to the absolute Being. Zwinglius had already set the example of this great innovation, which the "Reformed Church" sanctioned in its liturgies, in its worship, and in the works of most of its renowned theologians. *Christus, qua Mediator, non est adorabilis,* was one of the common positions of the Reformed dogmatic teaching which gave the most offence to the Catholics and the Lutherans.

The Holy Spirit completely corresponds in Calvin's idea with the indwelling of God in the universe.* It is no longer a person in the true sense of that word; it is the ἐνέργεια τοῦ θεοῦ of early times, or, so to express it, it is God in action in the world and in the soul. The Holy Spirit, says the *Confession of Faith* of Rochelle (art. vi.), is "the energy, power, and efficacy of the Father." How near is this to the most cherished idea of the religious philosophy of our own days, that of the divine power which exists in all things, and which causes the development of the universe!

Yet we must not imagine that the old "Reformed

* *Ubique diffusus, omnia sustinet, vegetat et vivificat in cœlo et terrâ.*

Church" had formally broken with the Trinitarian tradition. On the contrary, the Reformers always professed to follow it; they desired to defend it against its opponents; they boasted of their fidelity to the doctrine of Athanasius and Augustine; and they were sincere in their illusion. But when we penetrate below the surface, it is at once seen that the fundamental idea is changed. There is henceforth as great a desire to put prominently forward the real humanity of Christ as there had formerly been respecting his complete divinity. When the human consciousness of Christ is taken as the starting-point the centre of gravity of the system is displaced, the edifice of the old dogma totters; and therefore we do not hesitate to inscribe the *Protestant Orthodoxy* at the head of the period which sees the laboured erection of the divinity of Jesus Christ slowly falling. This orthodoxy is to Unitarianism what the Christology of the later Pauline Epistles was to the theory of the Word. The exact form of the idea is not yet discovered, but the idea itself is in course of evolution.

We are about to find in the bosom of the same Protestantism some innovators less respectful towards the Trinitarian dogma. The Catholic Church has nothing more to say upon the subject. Making, as it has done from the sixteenth century, a special claim of immutability, it has confined itself to sanctioning, by the Council of Trent and in the Romish Catechism, the doctrine of the *Quicumque* Creed. It is the divinity of Mary which is now steadily rising within its pale. That of Jesus will remain with its glaring contradictions, piously accepted by faith, which, moreover, among Catholic nations troubles itself but little about the claims of reason. When Bossuet wishes to express in his magnificent diction his manner of conceiving the Trinity, he resorts to the old, unsatisfactory comparison of the scholastic Anselm, that is, of the human mind making itself objective mentally to itself, and this for him solves the difficulty of the divine duality of the Father and the Son. As to the Holy Spirit, he confesses that, to understand properly its procession from the Father and Son he must wait for the "blessed vision" of the future life.* And yet a little further on he finds a created Trinity in the human mind, which *is*, which *knows*, which *wills*, in the unity of its substance;† a comparison made before his time by the Dominican Durandus of St. Pourçain in the fourteenth century, and revived in the sixteenth by the Reformed theologian Keckermann, which has, however, this among its other failings, that it ends in Sabellian Modalism.

* *Elévations sur les Mystères,* 2me Semaine, iv. and v.
† Ibid. vi.

CHAPTER IX.

ANTITRINITARIANS.—THE SOCINIANS.

The same arguments which had been brought by the Reformation against the Catholic doctrines concerning salvation, militated against the Catholic doctrine respecting the person of Christ. Their close connection was early perceived; and although the considerations which we have above alluded to prevented a bold and general application of the Protestant principle to the dogmas of the Trinity and the Incarnation, yet from the beginning there were Protestants who declared themselves decidedly Antitrinitarians. Such were L. Hetzer, J. Denck, S. Franck, and J. Campanus, in Germany, D. Joris in Holland, Claudius in Savoy, and others. The most heterogeneous elements, a cold rationalism and an ardent mysticism, pantheistic speculation and a tendency towards the simply practical, were frequently commingled in these earliest and somewhat tumultuous movements of advanced Protestantism.

It is a remarkable fact, confirming what we have already said, that the opposition to the doctrine of the Trinity was most frequent amongst the Protestants of those countries in which the Reformation was least popular, that is in Italy and Spain. The Reforming movement was there more peculiarly an intellectual one, and was consequently limited to the educated classes. The Protestants, emigrating from those two countries from fear of the Inquisition, arrived in France and Switzerland thoroughly imbued with heterodox conceptions as to the person of Christ. Amongst these men, very remarkable for their knowledge, if not for the depth of their views, stand prominent the names of Gribaldi, Blandrata, Alciati, Gentili, Ochino, Stankaro, and others, who all agreed upon the principle of the strict Unity of God, and rejected the Trinity of the Church. Michael Servetus was a Spaniard, a native of Arragon, one of those bold spirits who sometimes at once, and as if intuitively, seize hold of great and fertile truths, but are wanting in depth and in the sobriety of reasoning power requisite for the elaboration of a grand system.* To his misfortune, however, he sought to frame one. His system would have been forgotten, like many others of the time, if the lurid light of his funeral pile had not cast upon himself and upon his work that kind of lustre which, though it may not fascinate, draws attention by inspiring compassion in the beholder.

In his *Christianismi Restitutio* (1533), Servetus denied the Trinity of the Divine persons, calling it absurd and Tritheistic, a *Cerberus triceps*, and affirming that Jesus was essentially man. One might even say that his strong feeling against the Trinitarian dogma sometimes

---

* He appears to have been the first to discover the circulation of the blood ; at the same time he believed in judicial astrology, and passionately defended it against those who denied its truth. See *La France Protestante*, by Haag, art. *Servet*.

amounted to fanaticism. But not the less did he maintain the real union of God and man in the human person of Jesus. At this point his ideas become obscure and fanciful, though they are often most ingenious, and he is always very clear when merely opposing the old dogma. God, said he, is in Himself absolutely inaccessible to human reason, which can only speak of Him by negations. The only positive idea of the Creator which man could have would be one coming to him by a divine act of revelation. Now Christ was such pre-eminently, not an abstraction, but material, visible, real. Thus Servetus says that Christ is God; at least he is such so far as God can really exist for man *(quidquid habet Deus Christo inest substantialiter et corporaliter).* He could not admit a divine revelation apart from the sensible world. He held that above material and real beings there exists the ideal but abstract being, the *mens omniformis,* the *essentia essentians,* a kind of intermediary between God and reality; and that the principle of real being is light, which is at once material and spiritual, the unity of the ideal and the real, penetrating all things in various degrees. Christ is the luminous type-form in which the divine substance is reflected; he exists ideally in God from all eternity, and the man Jesus, with his fleshly nature, is the appearance in the real state of the being eternally begotten of the substance of the Father *(concedimus ipsam Christi carnem esse verbum Dei.—Caro ipsa Christi est coelestis, de substantiâ*

Dei genita. To this he adds the strangest physical theory of generation as proceeding from the union of the three male elements, water, air, and fire, with the female element, earth. It is very difficult to understand exactly what is meant by all this, and especially to see how it could be reconciled with the absolute transcendency of the Divine Being, which was the first postulate laid down.

We can easily conceive how objectionable this crude mixture of rationalism, pantheism, materialism, and theosophy must have appeared to the methodical and lucid mind of Calvin. Nothing was easier than to frighten pious souls by disclosing to them the list of dreadful doctrines uttered by the imprudent Spaniard, who dared to boast of *re-establishing* Christianity. The occasion was not lost. Servetus was burnt in effigy by the Catholic Court of Justice of Vienna from whose grasp he had escaped; and the Reformers of Geneva, with Calvin at their head, fell into the error which we must ever deplore, of rivalling in orthodox zeal the Papal tribunals. The punishment of Servetus would have passed unnoticed in a Catholic country, amidst many other still more terrible atrocities, but inflicted in a Protestant state it brought a sad reproach, and one which still remains.

Servetus, moreover, was not the only martyr of Antitrinitarianism. Campanus died in the prison of Cleves, Hetzer was beheaded at Constance, and Gentilis at Berne. Many others less known met with a similar fate, especially in places where the old Church, being still powerful though restrained by conventions or edicts, was glad of the opportunity to keep up the tradition of the persecution of heretics without exposing itself to the charge of attacking the Lutheran and Reformed Churches strictly so called. Still, Unitarian communities were established in Poland from the year 1563, with their principal centre at Racow. In Transylvania also, Blandrata, the physician to the reigning prince, obtained for the Unitarians official recognition.

In order to avoid useless repetitions, we shall pass on at once to the party which early gave its name to the scattered elements of the Unitarianism of the sixteenth century, and which, though small in numbers, and at least to all appearance in power, yet had immense influence upon the theology of the succeeding centuries. We speak of *Socinianism*, which, although of little value as a system, exercised an incalculable power as a dissolvent of the old dogma.

The Socini were natives of Sienna, and belonged to one of the bands of Italian refugees who emigrated to Switzerland. Lælius Socinus, notwithstanding his Anti-trinitarian views, lived peacefully at Zurich amongst the Swiss Reformers, in correspondence with Calvin and other Protestants of note, and in close intimacy with Bullinger. He was generally esteemed for his learning and character, although Calvin reproached him for his Arian and sceptical leanings. Private misfortunes hastened his end, and he died in 1562. His nephew, Faustus Socinus left Switzerland furnished with the papers and imbued with the ideas of his uncle, and settled amongst the Unitarians of Poland, of whom he became subsequently the most celebrated representative. His works and the numerous treatises collected in the *Library of the Polish Brethren*, which were much read notwithstanding the interdict laid upon them, are the principal sources in which must be sought the elements of the Socinian criticism of the Trinitarian dogma.

The first argument is, that the Trinity is a patent and crying contradiction. It supposes in the Deity three persons, distinguished from each other by individual and exclusive properties,—the Father by the absoluteness of his being, the Son by the qualification of having been begotten, the Holy Spirit by that of having proceeded; while it professes to remain faithful to Monotheism, and affirms that there is but one only God; which is the same thing as saying that three are equal to one, and one is equal to three. It is in vain for orthodoxy to take refuge in the idea of the mystery transcending human reason: its Trinity does not transcend reason, it subverts and disowns it. If reason must consent to such an abdication, it ought also to resign itself to the most grotesque religious absurdities. The repeated efforts of the Fathers and the Scholastics, by their successive failures, have only rendered the absolute contradiction of the orthodox dogma more evident.

None of those who have endeavoured to reconcile it, however subtile they might be, have been able to avoid either the Tritheism which denies the unity, or the Modalism which denies the persons.

In the second place, the orthodox dogma cannot stand against the idea of the Divine perfection. Is the property which makes each person distinct from the other two a perfection or an imperfection? If it is an imperfection nothing more need be said, for there can be no imperfection in God. If it is a perfection it is wanting to two out of the three persons.

The same stumbling-block exists in regard to the special relation of the Father and the Son. The dogma says that the Son is a Divine person, eternally begotten by the Father of His own substance. But what can be meant by this idea of generation in speaking of God? Again, God the Father possesses in Himself all perfection immutably. But if He begets another God exactly similar to Himself He is no longer absolutely perfect, for the existence of two absolute perfections side by side implies a contradiction.

The orthodox dogma further says that the Son, God infinite and perfect like the Father, became man, uniting in his single person the perfect divine nature with the human nature complete. Here, then, we have one subject, one double consciousness, knowing itself to be at once infinite and finite, perfect and imperfect, insusceptible of pain and yet suffering, incapable of sin and yet tempted, knowing all things and yet ignorant of many things, praying to itself and hearing its own prayers. Before the incarnation there were three Gods having the Divine nature in common, but nothing more. Since the incarnation a great change has taken place in the Deity; the human nature became henceforth inherent in it. Besides, if we are to understand this doctrine of the deity of Christ seriously, and not be satisfied with mere words, we must admit that the Creator of the universe was born in the condition of the human embryo, that he cried as an infant and was nourished at the breast of a woman, that he was subject to all the physical necessities of the bodily life, that he must have eaten, drunk, and slept, and that at last he was put to death by human hands. Will it be said that, in consequence of the distinction between the two natures, the man in Jesus alone passed through these vicissitudes, while the God remained exempt from them? If so, then how was Nestorius wrong in separating the two natures? And is it not evident that a second alternative stands pitilessly before us—Either the Man-God has borne or felt in his single personal consciousness all these human imperfections, and thus our whole criticism holds good, or the consciousness of Jesus was double; what one consciousness thought and felt was neither thought nor felt by the other, in which case we must say no more about the unity of his person.*

* The Socinians brought an analogous train of reasoning against the theory of the Arians. The Arian Christ, they said, is no more truly man

Again, it is said that the absolute deity of Jesus is necessary for the accomplishment of his work as Redeemer, since the infinitely outraged justice of God called for an infinite satisfaction. But, besides that innumerable objections may be made to this mode of viewing the redemption, it involves the same inextricable difficulty as before. Who suffered in Jesus, the God and the man at the same time? If so, God has made satisfaction to himself, which is absurd; and we have a God suffering and dying who is no longer God. Or if only the man suffered, what becomes of the infinite expiation which was supposed to be necessary?

Socinianism was reproached with contradicting the opinions of the Christian Church of all ages, and with reviving ancient heresies such as had been condemned in the early centuries. This reproach, which had some meaning when it proceeded from Catholics, was absurd when it came from Protestants, but it led the Socinians to study the history of the dogma of the deity of Jesus Christ. And though the doctrine appeared to them as obscure in its origin as it was to their opponents, they could at least show how common Unitarianism had been amongst the early Christians, and what a number of followers a Paul of Samosata, a Photinus, and others had

---

than is the orthodox Christ. They applied to both systems the same aphorism (Lib. Pol. Br.): *Nulla res, quæ una sit, duas formas essentiales habere potest, seu duæ res diversæ esse: jam enim non una, sed duæ res essent.*

obtained in the very times when Catholic orthodoxy began to triumph. Imperfect as it still was, the Socinian attack on this side successfully undermined the traditional prestige of the dogma, and sundered the tie of connection which the majority of Christians believed indissoluble between the existence of Christianity itself and the perpetuity of the belief in the Trinity.

Nevertheless, in conformity with the early Protestant method, the Socinians placed reasonings of this kind far below the arguments they drew from the Bible. They could with all confidence ask their opponents where the New Testament had taught the doctrine of the Trinity; in what passage Jesus had said that he was the second Divine person, and that he possessed two natures; and how they could explain, without doing violence either to their common sense or to their own system, the numerous declarations in which he absolutely subordinates himself to his Heavenly Father. They could call upon them to account for the precisely similar language used by his apostles, and they could point particularly to those passages in which it would be impossible to find the distinction of the two natures, such as Mark xiii. 32; John x. 36; 1 Cor. xv. 25—28; Heb. ii. 9, and others. In the two first chapters of our history will be found the substance of the arguments which the Socinians brought in abundance against the Trinitarian formulas. The exegesis of Calvin was their constant auxiliary, especially in many passages which doubtless refer to the unity between Jesus and God, but in which this unity is purely moral, and does not in any degree imply identity of substance.

Here, however, we touch upon one of the great weaknesses of Socinianism. It wanted the "historical sense." This defect, it is true, it had in common with the age; but it is more observable in their case, precisely because the Socinian was the one party most independent of tradition, and it had attacked orthodoxy principally in the name of reason. To conclude from this, as has been often done, that Socinianism betokens a decline in piety, is to calumniate a whole body of honourable men who displayed as much devotedness, and counted as many martyrs as any other religious communion. Still we must admit that the Socinian doctrine, apart from its criticism of orthodoxy, is somewhat poor and commonplace, too nearly resembling the vulgar rationalism of another period, and unsuited to our modern modes of thought from a certain rigid quality it has, a something mechanical and capricious, which replaces the difficulties of orthodoxy only with affirmations quite as embarrassing. And the defect is more manifest in it than in its rival because this clashes with its promises. Orthodoxy, at any rate, does not boast beforehand of conforming itself to reason.

Thus it was that Socinianism invented a method of biblical exegesis intended to reconcile reason with faith in the written revelation. It assumed the necessity of submitting to Scripture, but the real meaning of each passage is what reason determines—a simple mode truly of adorning rationalism with the colouring of docile faith! The reason which was called in to decide in the last resort upon biblical questions was just the Socinian reason; and such a principle distorted, not less than orthodoxy, both the letter and the spirit of the numberless texts which are neither orthodox nor Socinian. As a specimen of this compliant exegesis may be cited the Socinian explanation of the prologue to the fourth Gospel, which denies that the theory of the metaphysical Word is to be found there. If it is said that the Word was *in the beginning*, that means at the beginning of the evangelical history. Jesus is called the Word or the Logos because he was commissioned by God to proclaim to the world *the word* of truth. The Gospel says that "all things were made by the Word," that is to say, *all things* relating to the founding of Christianity;—and more to the same effect.

The Socinian Christology is not less singular. Jesus is man, that is one of its first principles; and it is to the honour of Socinianism that it said this boldly and without reserve at a time when that assertion, so easy to make in our days, led to persecution and death. But out of deference to the Biblical narrative Socinus nevertheless admits the miraculous birth of Christ, maintaining that that does not in any way alter his true humanity. This miraculous man was afterwards miraculously carried up locally to heaven by God, whose will it was to reveal to him the heavenly mysteries in order that he might speak of them to men from personal knowledge. For human nature left to itself can know nothing of divine things, and every truth must be **communicated to it from without by a supernatural revelation.** The province of reason is merely to recognize the authentic origin and the real contents of the revelation given. Jesus accordingly descended again from heaven and discharged his commission. After his death he once more ascended into heaven, and there, deified as a **reward for** his virtues, he ever **lives as** dispenser of the divine graces. **Socinus does not even** see any difficulty in calling Jesus, thus glorified, God, **and** in addressing prayer to him, as one to whom God has delegated his power. Upon this point pure Calvinism was more advanced than Socinianism; while Davidis, one of the followers of Socinus, protested against what seemed to him a new infringement **of Monotheism.** Finally, the Socinian doctrine, which maintained so stringently the **Divine absoluteness against** Trinitarian orthodoxy, did **not** scruple, in order to save *free-will*—to which, **in opposition to Calvinism, it attached** immense value—to **limit** the omnipotence and omniscience of God. The good qualities and the defects of Socinianism were combined in the manner in which it regarded the Holy Spirit. Whilst it triumphantly demanded of orthodoxy what could possibly be the meaning of *personality* as applied to the action of God upon the mind, the dualism to which the system was committed by its superficial notion of the natural relations between man and God, prevented it from seeing in the Spirit anything more than the mechanical, external gift of certain particular graces to such men as God judged to be worthy of them. Socinianism comprehended nothing of the idea of an indwelling presence of the Divine Spirit in creation and in the human soul. The *Deus ex machinâ* was its great expedient; and however rationalistic in its criticism, it was in its dogmatic views as supernaturalistic as orthodoxy—perhaps even more so.

These defects, which its eager opponents took pleasure in pointing out, prevented the propagation of Socinianism. The Socinians were very religious, but not so justly could that be affirmed of their system. Besides, the same causes which had maintained Trinitarian orthodoxy in the great Protestant Churches during the sixteenth century continued in force in the seventeenth. In Germany, Holland, England, and France the very existence of Protestantism was constantly threatened by the Catholic reaction, the weight of which was felt through nearly the whole of this period. In comparison with the sixteenth, it was a century of languor, of distrust of everything liberal in Church and State. The pinions of religious thought were heavily shackled by this fear of every movement contrary to the traditions. With regard to theological studies the seventeenth century was in modern times what the middle ages were in the general history of Europe, a time of stagnation, a scholastic period. The brilliant position of France under Louis XIV., great as it was in the provinces of military achievement and literature, was not calculated to hasten on the emancipation of the human mind. Not Protestantism only, and the nascent criticism of the Richard Simons, the Cappels, the Daillés, and the Blondells, but Jansenism also felt this. The English Revolution of 1688, which marks the time when the European power of Catholicism received a check from which it has never recovered, was an event of supreme importance in the history of religious beliefs. The age of Louis XIV. came then in fact to an end; the eighteenth century began, and with it new elements appeared which greatly modified the mental attitude and tendencies of the Christian world.

The work of reflection, however, and of religious inquiry, if retarded, was never completely interrupted. The masses, it is true, absorbed in the struggle between the greater Churches, manifested very little sympathy with anything that would have complicated this by increasing the points of disagreement. But there were many modest learned men, many laborious theologians and educated laymen who found themselves brought by slow degrees to entertain views not very Catholic upon the Trinity, and consequently upon the deity of Jesus Christ. The Socinian criticism hollowed out for itself a great number of obscure passages, the traces of which are now discernible only by the few who are familiar with the theological literature of the period, but which formed innumerable openings for the infiltration of heterodoxy on all sides.

Here, indeed, we see the real practical influence of Socinianism. As constituting a separate Church, it had neither great power nor long duration. After flourishing for a time in Poland, where it was professed by a large portion of the nobility, it succumbed under the blows of the Jesuit reaction favoured by Sigismund III., which was the cause and commencement of the misfortunes of that unhappy country. Socinus himself died in 1604, after having twice narrowly escaped death by the hands of fanatics. Unitarianism as a constituted Church had a very precarious existence in Transylvania, Prussia, and Holland. It is only in Transylvania that it has existed under that form until the present day. In that country, according to the last census, the number of Unitarians amounts to about fifty thousand. In England, where James I., so lately as in 1611, burned three Antitrinitarians at the stake, and where Unitarianism was always more remarkable for the character than for the number of its adherents, it was not until the last century that it was tacitly tolerated, and not until the commencement of the present century that it received civil recognition.*

* The history of English and American Unitarianism may be briefly summed up in the following particulars. The first Unitarian of note in

A more brilliant destiny awaited it in the New World. But, we repeat, the influence of Socinianism must not England was an Italian, J. Acontius, a refugee at the court of Elizabeth. The direct or indirect influence of Socinianism increased the number of Unitarians, of whom, in the middle of the seventeenth century, John Biddle was the chief representative. Notwithstanding the most unfavourable circumstances and some amount of real persecution, the progress of Unitarianism was so rapid, that Dr. Bull thought it necessary to oppose it in his weighty and famous *Defensio Fidei Nicænæ* (1685). English Unitarianism can boast of having been the faith of a Milton, a Locke, a Newton, a Lardner, a Priestley, a Price, a Holland, and others. But it was only in 1773, through the instrumentality of Theophilus Lindsey, that it was constituted into a distinct Church. It can now add to the celebrated names above cited those of Professors Martineau and Tayler, without mentioning numbers of distinguished scholars and theologians, such as Dr. Beard and his son, Gaskell, and many others. The Unitarians of England do not form a numerous body (386 places of worship and 339 regular ministers). This arises chiefly from the fact that their views are widely spread in other churches whose Unitarian members do not like to leave them. The Socinian and deistical influences also, to which English Unitarianism was subject in the past, have gained for it the reputation of being dry and cold, which still hinders many persons from joining its ranks. It is, however, unnecessary to say that it has by degrees pretty generally emancipated itself from all the narrow and strange conceptions of Socinianism. At the present day it is one of the elements in what is usually called *Liberal Protestantism*. It has moreover spread with marvellous success in America. From Boston, its principal centre, it has been diffused throughout New England and amongst the other States. Such names as those of Henry Ware, Channing, and Theodore Parker are in themselves sufficient to shed lustre upon a religious communion of such recent date. Even more than in England has it extended widely in America beyond the Unitarian churches properly so called, and especially amongst the Universalists, and in the Society of Friends. Without exaggeration, we may say that it is in fact the religion of the majority of enlightened men in the young republic. From it have sprung the great movements of philanthropy and social reform. The unity of God, Christ recognized as the revealer and the model of the true religious life, love as the essential attribute of God, and that which ought to constitute the essential quality of the Christian, such are the invariable characteristics of this remarkable system of religious thought.

by any means be measured by the number of its professed adherents. It was a leaven rather than a society, but a leaven wonderfully permeating the larger Churches. In the seventeenth century, Socinianism was undoubtedly the dread of the orthodox of all communions. Bossuet, like Jurieu, suspected it everywhere, and it was in fact working to some extent in all directions, not as a system, but as a tendency. Jurieu himself, the bitter but honest defender of the Calvinistic orthodoxy, admitted, to the great offence of Bossuet, whose favourite theories respecting the immutability of the traditional belief such assertions overturned, that "the mystery of the Trinity remained in an unformed state until the first Council of Nicæa, if not to that of Constantinople; and that the generation of the Son in time (not from eternity), shortly before the creation, and his inferiority to the Father, were taught by the Christian writers of the three first centuries."

If a Jurieu spoke thus, what heresies must have been concealed under the professed uniformity of Calvinism! One special characteristic of Unitarianism, at least in continental Europe, already presented itself, namely that it has very seldom shown the desire to organize itself in separation from the existing churches. It has accommodated itself readily to Protestant worship, especially that of the Reformed liturgies, and to the religious customs of the Protestant nations, always finding some divines and clergymen more or less cautiously in sympathy with it. And perceiving that the Protestant Church had only to become insensibly transformed in order to accept it fully, it has always contentedly resigned itself to the idea that, being the issue of learning and quiet reflection, it must patiently wait for the time when the Christian world will be sufficiently enlightened, and sufficiently emancipated from traditional prejudice to unite with it. It has frequently been condemned by synods, but nothing has been able to prevent its slow advance. In 1689, the Dutch theologian Roël could controvert, without serious consequences to himself, the eternal generation of the Son, declaring that it was a contradiction, and applying exclusively to the historical Christ the name of **Son of** God. It may be affirmed in general that the liberal tendency in the Reformed Church, though it never adopted the Socinian system as a whole, became more or less impregnated with its tendencies, and with its criticism of the dogma.

This was particularly the case in that fraction of the Reformed Church which, after having been condemned by the Synod of Dordrecht, separated from the general communion in the Low Countries, under the name of *Remonstrant* or *Arminian*. The cause of the separation, strictly speaking, was the repugnance felt by the disciples of Arminius to the Calvinistic doctrines of the radical corruption of the human heart, and of predestination. Beyond the Low Countries, Arminianism, without causing a schism, penetrated into most of the

Protestant churches. More timid than the Socinians, the Arminians did not usually venture so far as to assert the pure humanity of Christ. Their pious divines Episcopius, Limborch, and Curcellæus contented themselves with a theory of subordination, which very nearly resembled Arianism, or at least the doctrines taught by the Catholic Fathers of the third century. But this also was a dissolving agent in regard to the orthodox belief, a middle term which visibly tended towards heterodoxy. In the same country of Holland, which, in spite of temporary reactions amongst a people devotedly attached to Calvinism through patriotic feeling, was becoming more and more the classic land of religious liberty, was published the *Library of the Polish Brethren* (after 1656), with, amongst other works, those of a Socinian theologian, J. Crell, who sharpened against orthodoxy the already keen-edged weapons of Unitarian criticism. All these facts, and more which might easily be enumerated, prove that from the seventeenth century, notwithstanding the outwardly rigid forms of orthodoxy, the era of the absolute domination of the Trinitarian dogma had passed away never to return. Besides, theology was no longer alone in the study of transcendental questions. Its servant in the middle ages being now emancipated began to share with it the empire of mind. The modern philosophy had come into existence.

CHAPTER. X.

MODERN PHILOSOPHY.

MODERN philosophy, of which the patriarch is Lord Bacon of Verulam, is to the *a priori* metaphysics of the middle ages what the Reformation was to the ancient Church. The individual throws off the yoke of philosophical tradition, and stands face to face with the truth for which he feels himself to have been formed. Experience is henceforth, if not his only and constant guide, at least the first in order of time, and his supreme court of appeal. The new method was first applied to outward nature, but very soon also to the human mind and everything which concerns it. On this path philosophy and theology, for a time separated, were destined once more to meet.

But this meeting had yet to be waited for. As Luther had founded religious Protestantism by opposing his *credo, ergo salvor*, to the artificial methods of communion with God extolled by the middle ages, so Descartes founded philosophical Protestantism by opposing his famous *cogito, ergo sum*, to the Scholasticism of the past. Both thus kept clear of the gulf of religious nihilism and philosophical scepticism. Descartes was also like Luther in his fear of the consequent and firm application of his principle. His timidity in presence of the tradition of the Church is astounding. Although he admitted, on the one hand, that it is absurd for finite beings to seek to define the Infinite One, yet on the other, he still bent reverently before the dogmas "which it has pleased God to reveal," such as the Trinity and the Incarnation.* Neither Luther nor Descartes, altogether revolutionary as they both were, could entirely detach themselves, the one from the old monk, the other from the Breton Catholic.

Spinoza, the disciple and the true continuator of Descartes, was more courageous, and did not shrink from introducing his philosophical ideas into theology. It is clear that, brought into contact with the absolute substance of which all phenomenal existence is but a temporary mode, the dogmas of the Trinity and the Incarnation have no longer any meaning. Everything supernatural was at once dismissed. This principle which he applied with great freedom to the Bible led Spinoza to take decidedly peculiar and original views (some very true, some strange) of the miracles, the prophets, and the inspired writers in general. Jesus, though in his idea simply a man, is the pre-eminent revealer, not so much of intellectual truth, as of the religious truth necessary to the moral life, such as the existence and perfection of God, his justice and mercy, and the love of one's neighbour. By the eternal Son of God is not meant Christ, but the Wisdom of God, which manifests itself in the universe, and especially in the human reason,

* *Principes*, i. 24.

but above all in Jesus Christ. "As to what certain churches add as to God having taken upon himself human nature," he says, "I declare plainly that I do not know what they mean. It appears to me the same as if they were to pretend that the circle took upon itself the nature of the square."* In another place he calls Christ "the voice of God." If, in setting forth summarily Spinoza's theology, we could forget the meaning given by the premises of his system to the usual consecrated terms which he employs in speaking of God and His attributes, and of Christ, we might see in his religious doctrine only a kind of Unitarianism austere, philosophical, strongly influenced by the idea of the indwelling of God in the world and in the soul. But what becomes of religious realities when brought into connection with the unconscious "substance" which he calls God? How far this discordance between philosophical ideas and religious sentiments was perceived by the recluse of the Hague himself, I am still unable to say, though I have often reflected upon it with his works and the biographies of him open before me. To accuse him of any kind of hypocrisy would be to prove that we do not know him. Yet it is very difficult to suppose that he so far deceived himself as to the true significance of his doctrines, and it is scarcely likely that we should find one of the closest reasoners of modern times under an illusion leading him to combine religious sentiments

---

* Comp. the *Lettres à Oldenbourg*, 21, 23, and 25.

of great purity with speculative ideas calculated to destroy them.

Spinoza long remained isolated. His theology was even less known than his philosophy. Yet the latter sprang too directly from the essence of Cartesianism, and its logical force was too evident, for it to escape the observation of able thinkers. It was chiefly against his abstract idea of substance, as destructive of all "particular" and personal reality, that philosophy rose in arms; and with Leibnitz people readily believed that a subtile metaphysical doctrine was henceforth to be reconciled with the fundamental beliefs of orthodoxy. Leibnitz showed —and this was the idea truly original with him—that in active force was that essence of substance which Spinoza made to consist only in perfect sufficiency. From active force he derived motion, and from motion difference, or individuation. Substance in motion is individualized into *monads*, that is to say, into active forces, each in itself distinct from all the rest. The universe is a system of innumerable monads, which are all of a spiritual nature. Matter is only their appearance and their effect on each other, an obscure representation which they make for themselves of their simultaneous existence; in more modern language, a lower stage in the development of mind. The pre-established harmony explains the continuous agreement which exists in the living being between the superior monad, which is the soul, and the system of inferior monads which forms the body. These are like two watches which always indicate the same hour, thanks to the skilful foresight of the watchmaker who set them in motion. The idea of God, and that of this pre-established harmony coincide, and it is not easy to see in the God of Leibnitz anything more than the harmonic unity of the universe. Only, this unity is active, conscious, intelligent; and man holds with it a permanent and personal relation, which has nothing in common with the absorption of individuality in Spinoza's "substance."

But how will such a view of God agree with the ecclesiastical dogmas? Here it is that the genius of Leibnitz descends to the level of mere dexterity. Leibnitz was especially the philosophical conciliator. He sought to re-unite all, even the Protestants and Catholics, so that it was long a question to which communion he himself really belonged. It is now a matter of proof that, after much tergiversation, he remained a Lutheran, but it is also certain that personally he attached very little importance to Church differences. There was always much policy, and even diplomacy, in his philosophy. Bayle and Spinoza, whether he names them or not, are ever present to his thought, and determine the course of his ideas. Bayle had said* that the dogmas of the Incarnation and the Trinity destroy all certainty, by subverting the most evident axioms of human thought. Leibnitz took care

---

* *Diction.*, art. *Pyrrhon.*, *Rem. B.*

in his system of the universe, to leave open a door for the miraculous, and even for the contradictory; but for the contradictory under the title of the *supra-rational*. The point was therefore to prove that the dogmas attacked by Bayle, the Socinians, and Spinoza, were not contradictory, as at first sight might be supposed. But this ground was so barren, that Leibnitz himself could bring nothing new out of it. The Deity being, according to his view, above all things Intelligence, he, like Bossuet, though with a little modification, adopted the comparison conceived by Durandus of St. Pourçain, of the mind "acting upon itself in thinking of itself and of what it does." The Father is the *intellectivum*, the Son the *intelligibile*, and the Holy Spirit the *intellectum*. He says, however, in another place, "the Divine substance no doubt has privileges which exceed those of other substances."* For the honour of his logic, he would have done better to have confined himself to this last remark.

This forced and laboured character of any religious philosophy which strives to connect itself artificially with tradition where there is no natural agreement between them, was the character of all that school of Wolf which endeavoured to popularize the ideas of Leibnitz. Nothing could be less natural than Wolf's *Theologia Naturalis*, which appeared in Germany about the time when a religion equally *natural* began to

* *Remarks upon the Work of an English Antitrinitarian.*

flourish in France. It discovered nothing better than some trifling modifications of the trite comparison of the Trinity with the individual human mind, as if by that means a plurality of persons could ever be obtained without giving up the indivisible unity which constitutes essentially the mind of each individual.

These often-repeated efforts undoubtedly retarded, but they could not arrest, the decline of the Trinitarian dogma. Indirect causes, not as yet even thought of in the sixteenth century, and **scarcely** perceptible in the seventeenth, contributed to undermine it in the minds of the more enlightened, even of those not familiar with theological discussions. The dogma of the deity of Jesus Christ, as formulated by orthodoxy, served as a connecting link between God and the world, between heaven and earth. It did not depend, therefore, solely upon the idea which might be formed of God. Now **since** the time of Copernicus, Kepler, Galileo, and Newton, the views held with respect **to the world no** longer corresponded with the orthodox conceptions. There was an evident disproportion between the place given by ortho**doxy to** the history **of** God upon earth, and that which must be assigned to our planet in the immensity of space. **How** could it be thought that the great Being who sustains and directs the worlds scattered by millions through this immensity, had come **to** enclose his being in a human form, and **to** concentrate Himself upon a small globe that could not contain all the life in **the** universe? How could the idea be accepted that this infant Jesus, asleep on his mother's knee, was at the same moment governing the starry orbs which gravitate in the infinite heavens? Science, to use Diderot's expression, magnified God, while the orthodox theology contracted Him. There was a plain conflict. The two things no longer agreed. Moreover, to speak generally, the supernatural, already so greatly encroached upon by the Reformation, recoiled continually before a more exact knowledge of the laws of nature and of history. The human intellect became as untractable, as it had before been submissive, to the idea of the miraculous. Socinianism itself, still so imbued with supernaturalism, could no longer satisfy this condition of mind. And such had been the identity established by tradition between the Gospel and the orthodox doctrines, that the rupture with the traditional dogmas soon turned into an open hostility to Christianity.

It was in England, and by reaction against the extremes of Puritanism, that this hostility burst forth. Socinianism, deprived of its supernatural elements, necessarily led the way to positive Deism, in a country so utilitarian, in which religion is mainly regarded on its practical side, and mysticism is only popular if it assumes violent forms; where, when a revolt arose against the dogmas of the Trinity and the Incarnation, that tender indulgence was not felt towards their speculative forms which still maintains them in Germany.

But this very name of Deism which came to be applied to an entire school of thought, indicates the direct denial of the whole doctrine of the Church with respect to God and Christ.

Deism, in sound philosophy, is not tenable. It establishes a dualism, a real antithesis between God and the world, each standing distinct from, and so limiting, the other. The world is an old machine that was formed long ago, still working however very well, at least in its larger movements, and all our modern philosophical ideas of immanence, of organic development, of creative or intuitive spontaneity, would have appeared mere jargon, as they still appear to those who have not reached beyond the bare deistical conception. It was in this school, and in consequence of this void left in philosophy, that those theories were framed which were afterwards so popular in France; that attributed to the *priest*, to his selfish and politic calculations, or else to the artifice of legislators, everything lying beyond the narrow limits of so-called natural religion, that is, the existence of God, virtue, and a retributive immortality. Here, also, it is not surprising to meet frequently with views which, like those of Hobbes and Blount, favour the most absolute spiritual despotism, by turning religion into an arbitrary institution, intended for the people, who must receive it ready-made from the gracious hand of their sovereign. Jesus, according to this view, was merely "the lawgiver of Christians." Homage was ordinarily paid to the excellence of his moral teaching and the purity of his character, though not without imputing to him at times diplomatic calculations more befitting an English bishop in the House of Lords than the Prophet of the Galilean mountains. Herbert, Toland, A. Collins, Shaftesbury, Tindal, T. Chubb, and Bolingbroke, were the chief representatives of this school whose disciples assumed the title of *Freethinkers* but often proved that to call oneself *free* is not necessarily to be so. Occasionally, moreover, their anti-Christianity was more Christian than they themselves supposed. Some of them even flattered themselves with the idea that it was substantially the original Christianity of which they had recovered the title-deeds, by clearing it of false conceptions originated by the fancy of the priesthood from the very times of the Apostles. Even within the Church itself Deism, as a philosophical principle, counted many distinguished partisans. Locke thought himself perfectly Christian when writing his *Reasonableness of Christianity*, which made the essence of the faith to consist in believing in the divine mission of Jesus to enlighten men. His theory of the origin of ideas in sensation, and of the human soul as a blank sheet on which they were inscribed, and on the other hand his sincere piety, both together made him feel the need of a revelation *ex machinâ*, given from without, though nevertheless open to reason to verify its origin and to determine its tenor. This is almost **pure** Socinianism. In his time, as well as since, Unitarian views have largely prevailed among the Anglican clergy under this deistical **form**. The celebrated Samuel Clarke laid down a complete system of theology in which might be seen the old Arianism revived.

From England the deistic mode of thought passed into France, where from the seventeenth century it had some timid advocates, and Voltaire lent to it the incomparable brilliancy of his style and his wit. It was especially in France that it became revolutionary. The Reformation seemed for ever extirpated from the soil. The French intellect, which had long slumbered as to religious matters, suddenly awoke to see itself confronted by a Church full of abuses of every description, and defying in a most irritating manner both common sense and science to a degree never attempted by the Established Church of England; and while, with the English, Deism was never anything more than a mode of thought on religious subjects much relished by the upper classes, which soon disappeared under the influence of the great religious revival at the close of the century; with the French, on the contrary, among whom also it was at first encouraged by aristocratic refinement, it afterwards became the received opinion of all ranks of the people. Deism was the belief of most of the Revolutionists, and the majority of men in the middle classes have still to this day no other. It is common in France to confound this simply with the denial of Christianity; and certainly, if the pretensions of orthodoxy are well founded, and if Christianity consists essentially in a certain number of immutable dogmas—amongst them that of the deity of Jesus Christ—this identification of Deism with non-Christianity corresponds with the reality. It is moreover unquestionable that many of the most celebrated Deists of the eighteenth century made no secret of their aversion to Christianity, at least as they understood it. But it will be seen by those who adopt the view set forth in the first chapter of this work, and who comprehend that it is possible "to speak against the Son of Man without speaking against the Holy Spirit," that this confusion is based upon an error. It is the fact however that, generally speaking, the movement of thought in the eighteenth century erred through its defect of religion, as if the internal organ of faith had become debilitated and incapable of comprehending grandeur of a religious type, or of appreciating the charm of mystical aspirations. Take one example to illustrate this. When we think in these days of Voltaire's "*La Pucelle*," we not only feel disgust at the idea of this cynical caricature of the French national heroine, but we find it extremely difficult to understand how a man of so much genius could have made so great a mistake. There was decidedly a defect in the eighteenth century, an impoverishment in religious feeling which no one can deny who is not himself affected with it.

But when we have granted **all this, we** have still the right, nay, it is a duty, to remember that in **very** many respects the deistical philosophy of the eighteenth century was incomparably more Christian than the Church. What system which preceded it so broadly unfolded **the** banner of humanity? What system so believed in enlightenment, in justice, and the high destinies of man; or so well asserted the rights of the poor, for whom, since the time of Christ, so few have shed a tear? Was it the fault of Deism, or that of the Church, if Christendom infatuated with dogmatism had overlooked for centuries the fact that abominable horrors were perpetrated under the shadow of the Cross? At least one-half of those who at the present day treat it only with contempt or insult, owe to Deism the security of their lives and the liberty of their consciences. If **it** has sinned against the Divinity, the Christian Church, on the other hand, has too long sinned against Humanity to be justified in showing itself so haughty. **If** there is anything Christian and true in the Trinitarian contradictions, it is that the divine element and the human, so far from destroying each other, ought to unite harmoniously for the salvation of man. Now the Church for centuries had sacrificed the human element to the divine; and instead of heaping anathemas on those who have successfully restored the former to its rights, it would have done better to profit by the lesson of humanity which they taught, and thus to have become itself more truly

Christian. Perhaps the only service that the Ultramontane reaction has rendered us is, that it has brought us back to a juster appreciation of the last century. When we see re-appearing the shadow of the monsters with which the eighteenth century had to contend, while they were still full of life and vigour, we learn to estimate more highly its courage and the peculiar function it discharged, which we were but too ready to forget.

Besides, it is an exaggeration to say that the Deism of the eighteenth century was in principle hostile to Christianity. If in some of its representatives it degenerated even to folly, or went so far at times as to lose itself in gross Atheism, yet, as set forth by many others, it kept within the current of the grand Christian tradition, or rather gave to it a new development. D'Alembert would have welcomed above all things a Christianity purified and tolerant, moral rather than dogmatic.* Voltaire, in his better moments, when not possessed by the demon of satire, holds the same view, and it is not true that his *Ecrasons l'infâme* refers to the Gospel. He and Rousseau, but especially the latter, with whom the religious sentiment is more vivid and constant, and who in his *Vicaire Savoyard* suggests a new way in which to understand and admire the Gospel, were in the main Unitarians of a peculiar type, believing Jesus a man, but also willingly admitting the divine character, in the sense in which their Deism allowed them to

* See his article *Genève* in the *Encyclopédie*.

understand the term, of his mission and his moral teaching.

So much as this we can in these days affirm in the name of Christianity properly understood, without therefore closing our eyes to the grave defects of a spirit different from our own, and of a philosophy that has for ever passed away. The importance of Deism in connection with the present history consists in this, that by its influence the dogma of the deity of Jesus Christ began to decline amongst those nations which continuing in the ranks of Catholicism had been hitherto strangers to the new evolutions of religious thought. We may add that a similar movement, less brilliant but quite as popular, took place in Germany at the same time. The old Rationalism in that country corresponded to the French Deism, resembling it not only in its humane and tolerant character, but also in its absolute defect of the historical and critical sense, its superficial explanations, its easy satisfaction, and its antipathy to everything in any degree approaching mysticism. It differed from it in one respect, that it continued almost everywhere closely attached to the Church and to Christianity. It was pedantic, but laborious and learned, and to it we owe the first really scientific essays on the history of dogmas. It was, in effect, the successor of Socinianism, which re-appeared in it under a new form. To this commonplace Rationalism the Trinity could only appear as a long-continued aberration of Christian thought corrupted by Platonism, and the Incarnation as a doctrine borrowed from the Pagan religions. All the Rationalists doubtless did not go so far in their opposition to the old dogmas. Many adopted Arianism more or less revised and corrected as a reasonable and scriptural compromise. At Geneva in particular was this middle course adopted by the most highly esteemed professors and pastors. Still, deistical views prevailed and cast the doctrine of the Trinity into the shade, as much with the Genevese Bernet and J. Bonnet, who were in other respects so pious and so attached to the Church, as in the case of Reimarus and Bahrdt, who revolted completely from the Christian tradition.

Lastly, while we cannot dilate upon systems which had besides but little influence, we may just note that the mysticism of the middle ages of the pantheistic tendency was perpetuated in modern times by Schwenkfeld (d. 1569), Weitzel (d. 1588), and J. Bœhme (d. 1624), always continuing faithful, notwithstanding its numerous variations, to the fundamental idea that the orthodox dogma of the incarnation of God is nothing more than the abstract ideal expression of what is eternally taking place in the world and in man, where God is born and suffers in order to manifest his glory. Swedenborg, the greatest mystic of the eighteenth century, dated the era of the corruption of the Church from the Council of Nicæa, and vehemently contended against the doctrine of the Trinity, for which he substituted the idea of a personal God strictly One, who became man in order to present to faith a human and therefore a comprehensible object. This was still a kind of Unitarianism, under a form at once poetical and fanciful. When the hour for the decline of a dogma has struck, the most opposite tendencies appear to combine to hasten its fall. This decline, however, was not yet so complete as one might have believed at the close of the eighteenth century.

CHAPTER. XI.

THE NINETEENTH CENTURY.

NOT in religious matters only is the eighteenth century open to the reproach of having built much on the sand. It was its misfortune that, in the first ecstacy of emancipation, it did not perceive that the abuses and errors which required correction rested upon something deeper than the caprice or the interest of those who desired to maintain them. Its idea was that, were these but suppressed or rendered powerless, the good and the true must at once triumph. It was misled by what we may term its nominalism with regard to history, and by its own explanations, which were always based upon mere accident and contingencies. As to religion, indeed, it may be affirmed that, if we except the ideas of toleration which it spread universally even amongst the intolerant, the great modification which it introduced in the religious condition of the Catholic nations, and the spirit of distrust which it communicated to believers themselves as to the supernatural, it left everything very nearly as it was, while it gravely compromised the cause of emancipation itself.

A reaction was in fact inevitable, one which would of necessity be at once philosophical and religious, and of a kind to satisfy the wants that had been misconceived or suppressed. In philosophy, Deism could no longer stand against the objections of reason. In religion, every one was tired of optimism and hollow declamations. Deism removed God so far from the world and from humanity that piety was exhausted in its endeavour to find Him again in the cold heights of heaven, and it ended by abandoning the effort. Still, the eighteenth century had also its proper function, its legitimate, and to a certain extent invincible force.

Hence arises the double character, in the religious point of view, of the nineteenth century, which is divided between attempts to revive the institutions and principles which the eighteenth flattered itself that it had for ever uprooted, and the efforts of those who desire to complete its work, taking advantage of what was good in it, while keeping clear of its errors.

Thus have we in our century two theologies, the one

seeking to reinstate the old doctrines, and to maintain them as far as possible; **the other** assuming towards them an attitude similar to that which the experimental sciences of the present day hold to the **ancient** *a priori* systems, that of a science of observation, **so far** at least as religious subjects can be so regarded; in harmony therefore with the kindred sciences the acquired results of which are of a nature to throw light upon it.

From the close of the eighteenth century philosophy **acquired** greater seriousness and depth, **and** since that time, wherever set forth **with any** weight of authority, it has very rarely shown in presence **of** Christianity and the Church the ill-humour which characterized the majority of its representatives **in the** previous period. It was with Kant that the new philosophy began. He inherited from the eighteenth century its sceptical, distrustful spirit; but he brought it to **bear** upon **that** century itself **as** upon every other. The deistical reasoning was submitted by this powerful thinker to a merciless criticism which almost reduced it **to** nothing. But he **also** put **an end to that over-free** style **of** expression which disfigures many **of** the so-called philosophical productions of the same century. No longer was **bold** thinking to procure acceptance by pandering **to** sensual tastes. Utilitarianism and enjoyment must give place to the *categorical imperative*. Rigid morality resumes its rights, and it is on the moral ground, carefully cleared of every poisonous **growth, that** Kant re-establishes the religious truths which he believes unattainable by other methods. The Trinity itself he interprets as a symbol of moral truth. The God of Kant is conceived in a three-fold manner as legislator, governor, and judge, in accordance with the triple fact that there is within us a good principle, that this good principle can control the evil, and that it does in fact exercise this domination. Christianity he considers to be divine, not as a supernatural revelation, but as a higher morality. He looks upon the personal Christ in the same manner.

All this was perfectly in its place in the Kantian system, but it could only flourish and pass away with it. One might even already reproach the philosopher of Königsburg with the fault, so common after his time in Germany, of distorting the traditional formulas so as to make them convey ideas utterly foreign to their original meanings. But the respect of such a man for these relics of another age shows how the sympathy of earnest thinkers was returning to those dogmas which but lately were regarded with so much contempt. Besides, the philosophy of Kant was equally admired by the rationalists and the supernaturalists who were contending for the empire of mind in Germany, and it did nothing towards restoring anywhere the traditional faith. Christ the pattern of men by his holiness, was the doctrine common to all the theology which originated with Kant. Upon such a basis it was impossible to build either the divine, eternal generation of Christ, or his pre-existence, or even his miraculous conception.

The reaction, however, against the eighteenth century increased. Men did not believe in the old dogmas, but they began to find them poetical, rich in meaning, popular symbols of higher truth. This æsthetic view was represented especially by the learned De Wette, whose exquisite taste and feeling transfigured what was so often commonplace and poor in the old rationalism. The dogma of the Incarnation, for instance, was but the symbolic expression of the religious sublimity of Jesus —a view quite in accord with our own: the present work indeed begins by giving full prominence to the sentiment in which this dogma had its origin. But then we must remark that he who thus perceives the truth under the symbol can henceforth look upon orthodoxy only as the religion of the ignorant.

Yet such was the power of the reaction in favour of the past, that the boldest philosophers chose to wrap themselves in an orthodox mantle which fitted them very ill. Schelling, in unfolding his favourite principle of the identity of the ideal and the real, came to the conclusion that the pure ideal knows itself by eternally becoming reality; but that at the same time it is only absolute in its reality by grasping again the consciousness of its ideality. Thus we have the three principles in which Schelling recognizes the Father, the Son, and the Holy Spirit of the *Quicumque* Creed.* In the same manner Hegel says that God is Mind, whose pure activity is knowledge. Now this divine knowledge supposes an object known, and this is the eternal generation of the Son from the Father, or, so to express it, the universal "becoming." But if at first it distinguishes itself from this object, the mind afterwards recognizes it as identical with itself. Thus is the Trinity, in its simple elements, the pantheistic synthesis of the eternal antithesis, and an anticipation of Hegelianism. Could Athanasius or Augustine ever have believed it?

The true and fertile idea was, to substitute the world for the Son as the eternal object of the activity and love of the Divine Father; but by that very conception the ecclesiastical Trinity was shattered into a thousand pieces, and this people were unwilling to recognize. At the distance at which we have already arrived from the powerful movement which carried Germany away during the first quarter of our century—during the time when, full of youth and daring, but harassed to death by the

* In the later years of his life Schelling developed, as we know, a new philosophy of the absolute, which, according to its promises, was to approach still more nearly to orthodoxy. Still, so far as regards the Trinity this approach seems to have consisted in the substitution of the *drei Potenzen* for the three principles of his earlier teaching; but the gain to orthodoxy from this change is very doubtful. This last fruit of the thought of the old philosopher too desirous to pay court to the powers established, has generally been considered as a kind of dried fruit, incapable of perpetuating itself.

revolution, she clung to old institutions with the same ardour with which she threw herself into the most audacious novelties,—we can scarcely picture to ourselves how such mere displays of ingenuity could have been regarded seriously by a whole generation. But whatever may be thought of the philosophical value of these systems, it is in any case evident that they lead us far away from the ecclesiastical orthodoxy. Yet the Hegelian right wing sounded its trumpet everywhere, to announce to the world at large that it was body and soul Trinitarian in the most orthodox sense, and that it despised supremely from the height of its dressed-up orthodoxy all past, present, and future heresies. Marheinecke, Weisse, Gœschel, and others indulged themselves in this vein to their heart's content, to the great joy of the politico-religious reaction which saw at length "the wisdom of the world, the proud pagan, make its confession and submit itself humbly to the baptism of the Christian faith." But dreams that are too sweet do not last long. Strauss with one stroke of his pædagogic ferule chased away the swarm of illusions, and discovered to the eyes of the astounded faithful the serpent, full of life and venom, which the Hegelian right wing offered to the innocence still wrapped up in orthodox swaddling bands. The pitiless dissection which he made of these abortive attempts at the speculative re-construction of the Trinitarian dogma, is one of the most successful parts of his work entitled, *Die Christliche Glaubenslehre.*

The doctrine of the Incarnation had been similarly treated. In the view of Fichte, the Word becomes flesh in every man who is conscious of his unity with God, and who divests himself before God of all egoistical or individual pretension. In Schelling's, the incarnation of God is eternal, and is manifested in the tendency of nature to realize the absolute by and in humanity. According to Hegel, the Church teaches under a popular form what philosophy teaches under a scientific form; namely, that the "becoming" of the world is the continual incarnation of God, and that the human mind, when completely developed, ceases to regard God as a foreign, external being. No doubt there is in all this a theological truth more or less implied, that Christ can be and is no other than the religious man in his highest state of pure religiousness. But who could fail to perceive at the foundation of all these theories the humanity of Jesus in the Unitarian sense, at least if it is sought to bring them to bear upon the real history? And did not Strauss carry out the system to its true logical issue when he declared that, according to the Hegelian principles, the perfect Christ must be, not a man, not in any sense a type of the species, but humanity in the totality of its historical development?

Nevertheless, the orthodox reaction gave up in no wise its research in the arsenals of the new philosophy for the means of furbishing its damaged armour. Only, becoming less and less restrained by philosophical methods of thought, it adhered continually closer to the ancient dogmas, until it found some still more courageous adherents who could without shrinking repeat the *Quicumque* Creed from the first to the last word. The political powers were almost everywhere delighted with this return to the old doctrines, which promised golden days for the absolute princes; and what had been exceedingly worthy of respect in the first manifestations of the orthodox reaction, when it rose up in defence of piety that had been scoffed at, and in the cause of hearts thirsting for God, disappeared in proportion as, both in Church and State, one of the requisite conditions for attaining honours and lucrative places was to make ostentatious professions of orthodoxy.* Of the value of

* Of course in general statements like these, allowance must be made for sincere convictions, which no one, excepting for peremptory reasons, has any right to question, even with regard to those who profit the most from their way of looking at things. It must be understood that a time of transition like ours is also necessarily, and with the best intentions, a time of compromises. A remarkable illustration of this is presented by a singular theory of the incarnation which has had some little vogue during the last few years, and which has the advantage of being at once orthodox and Unitarian. Connecting itself with the Lutheran idea of the *exinanition* of the Word incarnate, this theory teaches that the Son, on becoming man, completely denuded himself of all his divine attributes, and even of his consciousness that he was divine, so that he had from the first, and even up to the eve of commencing his ministry, simply a human consciousness. It was only by degrees that, without losing this human consciousness, he recovered the sense of his divinity. Thus the passages in the Gospels which Unitarianism brings forward, and in which orthodoxy finds a difficulty, are explained, and those also, particularly in the fourth Gospel, which Unitarianism does not explain. In other words, Jesus believed for thirty years that he was only a man. The day came when he discovered that he had

such reactions posterity is always the best judge. The cannon of Sadowa, as also, alas! the cannon of Sedan and of Paris, have so changed the political and religious condition of Germany, that we must now await what the new era which is opening upon the young Empire has in reserve for the orthodox reaction. It may be affirmed from the merest general observation that, if the Governments were, or still are, enamoured of orthodoxy, a large majority of the German people are so no longer. But the fact is a serious one that the military passion, and a utilitarianism which hypocritically disguises itself under the mask of higher principles, are increasingly taking the place of that idealism and of that scientific delight in studies of the antique which formed the chief glory of modern Germany. The struggle against Ultramontanism is very important politically, but it has little bearing on religious thought.

In France things took a similar turn, but one less philosophical and of more immediate effect. There was no necessity, as in Germany, to restore one after another the chief dogmas of orthodoxy. The grand thing was to interest feeling once more in favour of the Church which claimed to be infallible. If once the authority of the Church is accepted, all the rest follows.

---

been completely mistaken with regard to himself, that his self-knowledge was grievously at fault, and that in reality he was a God. Either we have quite deceived ourselves, or such fancies are to dogmas what dotage is to human life, a sign of irremediable senility.

Romanticism and scepticism equally contributed to the religious reaction, the former by its infatuation for the middle ages, the latter by making more deeply felt than even the philosophy of the last century had done the void left in the soul by the loss of the Catholic faith. To believe everything or nothing, was the terrorist dilemma of the religious reaction. Except during short intervals, when the true spirit of the Revolution resumed its legitimate ascendency, the Government thought it prudent to ally itself with the clerical movement. The second half of the nineteenth century is reaping the fruits of the seed thus sown during the first half, and it is very difficult to make precise distinction between the artificial elements which enter into the composition of the Neo-Catholicism, and the legitimate elements arising out of the religious need of souls that could not be satisfied with mere Deism. Who can tell whether in some cases both may not be found together? One thing is certain however, namely, that the Catholic reaction has neither done nor produced anything as regards the dogma, the history of which we are now bringing to a close, to show that its continuous decline has been to any serious extent arrested.

We need not dilate upon the non-religious tendencies which after a fashion of their own follow in the steps of the eighteenth century, and for which the re-appearance of the old religious tyranny, which had learned nothing and forgotten nothing, created quite an autumnal blooming. In Germany M. Feuerbach conceived that the essence of religion was to be found in the worship that man renders to himself before the idealizing mirror of his own mind; and as a German atheist has always a mystical side, he reduced the Trinity to the ideal of the family, composed of the *father*, the *son*, and the *mother*. (In his opinion Mary ought to have been put in the place of the Holy Spirit.) The strange thing is that people always like to view themselves in a mirror that beautifies them, even when they know that the mirror is a flattering one; but, if the theory of M. Feuerbach is adopted, this self-adoration immediately ceases. In other words, religion vanishes when it has no longer any real *object*; and a sound philosophy, as we think, ought to infer from the reality of religion in the soul the reality of its necessary object. In France we have not all yet emerged from the ingenious conjecturing of the school of Dupuis, which assigned the same origin to Christianity and to Paganism, making of Christ a sun and of the apostles a constellation. The passionate materialism of some of the learned, and the Positivism, at times fanatical, of others, prove that man deprived of God needs some idol instead. Many will only adore the abstract ideal; that is, they worship the Divinity while disowning God. The Dutch have a very true proverb: *Natur boven de Leer, Nature is above doctrine.* It is for this reason that all such tendencies of thought are doomed to fail, as everything must that is contrary to the natural constitution of man; we merely glance at them in order to omit nothing: they evidently offer no contribution to the history on which we are engaged.

Much more significant in our view is the slow but continuous formation of what may be called modern Christianity, or Christian Theism, which is proclaimed and spreads with an increasing power, profiting by all the serious labours of science, attracting to itself the sympathies of the sincerely religious deists, and daily gaining recruits from the orthodoxies of the past. The great genius who may be considered the initiator and prophet of this modern Christianity in the last century was not a theologian by profession. It was Lessing who first clearly distinguished between the faith *of* Jesus Christ, as he himself spoke concerning himself in the Gospels, and the faith *in* Jesus Christ as deified by the Church. He also first saw that there was a Christianity of the spirit emancipated from the letter as well as from the priesthood. This Christianity is profoundly and necessarily Unitarian, although Lessing had also his speculative Trinity, which came to this, that the thought of God being necessarily creative, the Son begotten of the Father represents creation in its virtual perfecting. The idea is a fertile one, which has not been lost.*

His clear intellect was nevertheless for a time un-

---

* See in the *Bibliothèque de Philosophie Contemporaine* the article entitled *Le Christianisme Moderne-Lessing*, by M. E. Fontanès.

noticed in the attention that was given to another mind not less penetrating than his own, but more attracted towards the forms of the past. Schleiermacher, with his pure religious sentiment and subtile reasoning, elaborated a Christian doctrine in which mysticism and rationalism were conjoined. The Christ of his theology is the man without sin, whose divine glory the miraculous birth, the resurrection, and the ascension symbolically set forth, who has shed, and is always shedding in humanity by means of the community of his faithful followers, that spirit which delivers from sin and unites to God. Unfortunately Schleiermacher, from pure reaction against the barrenness of Rationalism and Deism, showed himself excessively complaisant towards the old dogmas. He did not accept a single one of them in its true import, and yet he so managed that all the old phraseology came once more into vogue. Besides, he attributed to Jesus a character so perfect, so superhuman, that it involved the necessary return to the idea of a miraculous Christ in the full force of the term. The human Jesus, the Christ of history, disappeared anew in the halo of an ideal being, a being historically impossible, and one who in the actual result was neither man nor God. His most eminent disciples followed and surpassed him in this course, the attractions of which we have above pointed out. In their writings the Christian sentiment and the Christian consciousness served to designate a multitude of ideas the merit of which consisted solely in their orthodox sound; and, under the name of a *theology of mediation*, the school of Schleiermacher elaborated heavy dogmatic lucubrations which are no longer read, and have been justly doomed to oblivion. Shall we give a specimen of these attempts to reconcile the irreconcilable? This is the way in which some of these representatives of the school set themselves to restore the divinity of Jesus Christ. God, it is said, is perfect. Now God's perfection must be that of love. But in order that the love of God may be real and perceptible to us, God must have *devoted* Himself. Only thus can we say that He is love, and love Him ourselves. Jesus then is God, and his suffering is God's self-devotion. The authors of this theory do not once appear to have remarked that the heroism of self-devotion arises from the victory gained within ourselves by duty over our selfish inclinations, and that without these self-devotion would not exist, or would signify something quite different. So that, if we must seriously accept the idea of a God who devotes Himself, we must also allow in the Deity the elements of egoism and of that lower nature without which there can be no question of self-devotion. It was a lame theory devised to help out a false position!

But the work of Schleiermacher was not limited to these unfortunate attempts at conciliation. The grand movement of religious and free criticism, the best product of modern Germany, is also connected with his name. The religion of the Christian heart, that is of the heart possessed by the ideal revealed in Jesus, was, from the time of the eloquent preacher of Berlin, the inspirer and director of those noble studies which have revived the knowledge of Christian antiquity. Faith, upon the ground to which it was raised by him, found itself too far above questions of interpretation and history to fetter henceforth the judgment of the learned and impartial Christian, while at the same time it shed over these difficult researches the charm inherent in whatever is related to it. The school of Tübingen came in its turn, and it is from this combination of influences that the modern Christianity, liberal, Unitarian, very little inclining to the supernatural, takes a vitality which in due time will secure its triumph; a triumph which will also be that of the sixteenth and eighteenth centuries, corrected by the nineteenth.

If it be a profession of Hegelianism to see in the mutual contradiction of the principles which govern a community the spring moving that community towards a higher point of view in which the opposing elements are overpassed and reconciled, we frankly avow ourselves to be so far Hegelian. This is very certainly the law of history attested by all the grand conflicts of humanity. But while this is recognized, it should not be forgotten that the two terms of the antithesis are never equal in the reconciliation they presage. One of them conquers, or, to vary the expression, is more decisively affirmed in the synthesis, while the second only comes into it partially denied and diminished. If then we ask ourselves, in the light of this principle—which will gain the day in the domain of religion, the emancipation begun at the Reformation and continued to the eighteenth century, or the orthodox reaction of our own days, we think we can affirm that the liberal principle has suffered, and still suffers, from the defects which have allowed its adversary to regain in the minds of men a position which seemed to be lost; that consequently it is bound to meet those demands, the justness of which alone explains their revival; but that nevertheless it is the liberal principle which will prevail. The extravagances of the opposite principle can only hasten its triumph.

The emancipation from all traditional authority was in the eighteenth century too little religious, and too disdainful of that very tradition whose superannuated yoke it desired, and with good reason, to break. It did not understand how productive is the method which fulfils rather than abolishes. It destroyed rather than reformed. Instead of correcting the tradition by purifying it, it claimed to secure the happiness of mankind by displacing it from its normal and regular development. I admit that it was driven to this by almost irresistible circumstances, but that is not the question. The fact is that it was so driven. Liberalism will become really victorious over its opponent only when it is as much or more religious.

We are not here so far from our general subject as might be thought. Henceforth the history of the dogma which we are considering will depend much less upon the controversies of which it may be the subject, than upon the choice which general opinion shall make between liberty and bondage. It is evident that, to most minds, the belief in the dogma of the deity of Jesus Christ is a question of predisposition to orthodoxy or to heterodoxy. Whatever weakens the prestige of orthodoxy, whether Catholic or Protestant, weakens also this belief. It no longer stands erect by itself. The Socinian criticism gave it its death-blow, and thenceforward it has declined. Amongst Protestants, the number of Unitarians, whether professing or non-professing, is immense. They are to be met with everywhere, even in the churches most celebrated for their conservatism. It is barely a possible thing still to meet with orthodox Protestants who venture to make adhesion to the traditional dogma a condition, *sine qua non*, of the Christian character. Many even allow themselves to introduce into it elements extremely heretical which alter its nature.* We see returning in their

---

* For example, M. Guizot, who, in his *Méditations sur le Christianisme*, without suspecting that he is sanctioning the Unitarian doctrine, explains the dogma of the Incarnation by laying it down that there is something divine in every human soul.

order Apollinarism, **or** the subordinated triad of the third century, and **even** Arianism. The general Synod of the " Reformed" Churches of France, which met in 1873, and the majority of whose members were animated by an orthodox spirit, did not venture to inscribe the Trinitarian doctrine amongst the articles **of** faith it deemed indispensable. The dogma is decomposing by **the** contrary process to that of its formation. The causes which were already destroying the orthodox faith in the eighteenth century are constantly in operation, and now more powerfully than ever. It is not only the **physical** world the constitution of which, as scientifically verified, no longer accords with the heaven of **the** Trinity, but history and criticism have confirmed the revelations of astronomy. The comparison of religions and of races no longer allows Christianity **to be set in** opposition to other religions as absolute truth against unqualified error. This comparison, while bringing to clearer light the superiority of the Gospel, has also **proved** that the law of development reigns here as elsewhere. The sole factor that breaks its regular rhythm is individual inspiration or genius, which sometimes allows one consciousness to move the moral world by **the** energy of its own sense of God. The history **of** the Christian dogmas no longer remains to be written. **The** Germans have written it, and if it still admits of improvement, it has produced such positive results that there **is no** further possible room for uncertainty as to the origination and the variations of the Trinitarian dogma. A Bossuet himself could not contest this, and if he still desired to defend his Catholic faith, he would take good care not to start with his radically false axiom, that the characteristic of the truth is to have been perfect from the beginning. It is evident that if the deity of Jesus Christ were essential to Christianity, as so many still imagine, this dogma would not have a distinct history, as we venture to affirm that it has. Biblical criticism, whatever progress may be still before it, has at least enabled us to find once more the truly human form of the historical Christ behind the cloud of legends and dogmas; a form of wondrous beauty, but not that of the second person in the Trinity. Hence have appeared in our time *Lives of Jesus*, a kind of work unknown before, or nearly so. And notwithstanding their defects, whether they have been too little scientific, as that of Neander; too negative, like the first, and even the second, of Strauss; too æsthetic and fanciful, as Renan's; or over-cautious, like those of Schenkel and Keim,— the common result is historical, human, positive. All these considerations, it is true, apply more to the Protestant than to the Catholic peoples; but liberty is one, though its development may vary for a longer or shorter time. Among Protestant nations religious emancipation has prepared the way for political freedom; among the nations that are Latin in religion and language, political freedom will bring in its train religious emancipation.

It would be to go beyond our programme and our ability if we terminated this historical sketch by an exposition of what appears to us to constitute the religious truth which is destined to triumph in the future. One should always be modest in any attempt to predict. There are some in these days who believe that all religion must pass away. To our eyes this excess of negation, like the excess of superstition which makes so much noise at the other extreme of the world of contemporary thought, is only, like that, spasmodic, and it will cease with the particular circumstances which have given rise to it. The hearts of men will not change at the bidding of any system whatsoever. The religious needs of the human heart guarantee the perpetuity of the seeking after God, that seeking which, according to the fine idea of Pascal, implies that He has already been found. To deny the legitimacy of religion is to commit a sin against nature. If, then, we would listen to the revelation of human nature, we must continue, or we must again become, religious; and if we would conform ourselves to the revelation of history, we must be assured that in regard to religion nothing can be established, nothing of any worth accomplished, if we absolutely break with the past.

Christendom has exhausted all the resources which it could derive from the faith *in* Jesus. It must return to the faith *of* Jesus, illustrated by the experience of eighteen centuries, to his sense of sonship to God; and, while giving to the Son of Man the place which rightfully belongs to him as the head and initiator of the faith, it must be inspired by his religious principle, bringing it to bear upon the world, upon the soul, and upon society, which has been so little touched by dogmatic Christianity. The dogmas of the Trinity and the Incarnation, formed by Catholicism, modified by the Reformation, dissolved by the Socinian criticism, unacceptable to reason, and contradicted by history, have had their day, and the elements of truth which they contain must be clothed in other forms, and enter into a different conception of things. For the God of the Trinity must be substituted the only God, above and within the world, who pours out in the immensity of time and space the inexhaustible riches of his power, whose eternal word is the universe, the revelation of his thought, the expression of his wisdom, the perpetual gravitation of the created spirit towards the creating Spirit from whom it proceeds, who loves it since He attracts it, and towards whom the creatures rise by a mysterious ascent. The union of the divine and the human exists potentially in every human soul. Jesus is supremely great because he, of all the children of earth, felt this union in his own person to be so intense and so intimate that, without for a single moment closing his eyes to the miseries of our race, he could give to God no other name than that of Father. It is not by the authority of a supernatural dogma, but by appeal to the history of the world, that we are permitted to say that man is, among all creatures, **the** adopted son of God. In him, in fact, creation becomes religious, and it is in this unique and marvellous phenomenon that we must seek our titles of nobility and the revelation of our higher destiny. Mysticism is in the wrong when it aims to impose on the reason its often arbitrary and contradictory dogmas. **But as a** presentiment of things that are ineffable, as a prophecy **of the** future, as a stammering utterance of words which are clearly spoken only in regions **yet** unknown, it is sublime, **it has its sacred** rights, and those are **to** be pitied whose ears remain always closed to its sweet modulations. There **is** wanting in them **a sense,** the sense of **the divine.** But those also are in the right **who** would **not have** man become enervated by suffering himself to be soothed continually by mystic chants. The religion which leads us to hope for heaven also bids us to labour on earth for the realization of **God's plan. Already** has the past witnessed **important and** blessed applications of the Christian principle of the Divine Fatherhood, and the human **brotherhood.** The **future ought to see such** applications **still more** complete, **and** in yet larger number. **The division** established by the middle ages between social life and religious life, that division which required that one should quit the world **in** order to follow some religious order *(pour entrer en religion)*, which was vanquished in principle by the Reformation, ought to give place to the absorption of one of the two terms by the other. Our ideal has changed. The saint of our days is no longer the hermit or the monk. It is he who devotes himself to the good of others; it is the liberator, the philanthropist, the great and good citizen. Henceforward it is *religious* and *Christian* to give one's-self up to the pursuit of science, art, poetry, politics. All depends upon the spirit one brings to them. Either the Christian principle that the human spirit is in essential affinity with the Divine Spirit has no meaning, or we must acknowledge that everything which contributes in man and in society towards living by the spirit and in conformity to the spirit, is according to the will of God, and in substantial harmony with the Gospel. It is a profound transformation of the religious idea that is now beginning, but this comes in logical sequence to its evolutions during the last three centuries, and it is connected with the fundamental thought of Jesus. Let men fear nothing for the glory of the Son of Man. It is to him, to the divine ideal living in him, that we owe our sense of sonship to God. In his pure heart have man and God mutually loved. This is the crown which no one will take from him.

www.ingramcontent.com/pod-product-compliance
Lightning Source LLC
Chambersburg PA
CBHW031956230426
43672CB00010B/2177